WILLIAM CAXTON

In the Same Series

LORD LISTER
By Cuthbert Dukes

SAMUEL BUTLER
By C. E. M. Joad

QUEEN ELIZABETH
By Gwen John

WILLIAM HARVEY
By R. B. Hervey Wyatt

MICHAEL FARADAY
By Wilfrid L. Randell

MARY WOLLSTONECRAFT
By Madeline Linford

WILLIAM CAXTON
By H. R. Plomer

OLIVER CROMWELL
By Andrew H. Dakers

CAPTAIN JAMES COOK
By M. Storm Jameson

SIR THOMAS GRESHAM
By F. R. Salter

JAMES WATT
By T. H. Marshall

RICHARD MARTIN
By Wellesley Pain

SIR THOMAS MORE
By G. R. Potter

THOMAS PAINE
By F. J. Gould

THOMAS CARLYLE
By Mary Agnes Hamilton

WILLIAM BYRD
By Frank Howes

FRANCIS BACON
By I. Levine

SIR EDWIN CHADWICK
By Maurice Marston

WILLIAM CAXTON

THE ROADMAKER SERIES

WILLIAM CAXTON

(1424-1491)

By

HENRY R. PLOMER

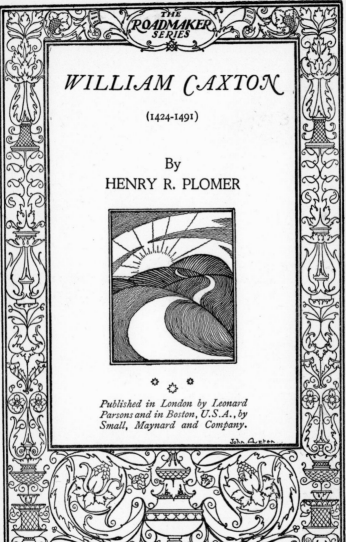

Published in London by Leonard Parsons and in Boston, U.S.A., by Small, Maynard and Company.

John Austen

First Published in 1925 by Leonard Parsons Ltd., and Printed in Great Britain by The Northumberland Press Limited, Newcastle - upon - Tyne

By the same Author

A SHORT HISTORY OF ENGLISH PRINTING

ENGLISH PRINTERS' ORNAMENTS, ETC.

CONTENTS

CHAPTER IV

CHAPTER V

CHAPTER VI

CHAPTER VII

CHAPTER VIII

CHAPTER IX

PREFACE

WHEN I was asked to write a Life of William Caxton for the Roadmaker Series, it seemed to me to offer an opportunity for dealing with the subject from an entirely new standpoint.

The most exhaustive of modern biographies of England's first printer is that of William Blades, and it touches every side of his character and work, and will always remain the standard authority on all that relates to Caxton. At the same time a very large part of Blades' work is purely technical, consisting of a survey of the art of printing, its history and its methods, as well as of particular descriptions of the various founts of type used by Caxton between 1474 and his death in 1491. He also gives interesting and valuable bibliographical notes about the books. The late E. Gordon Duff, who was the greatest living authority on English printing of the fifteenth and sixteenth centuries, in his *Life of Caxton,* written for the Caxton Club, confined his attention chiefly to the bibliographical side of the printer's work, and gave us faithful descriptions of the size, the number of leaves and the typographical particulars of each book or fragment of a book with gossipy anecdotes as to their rarity, their various owners and their present whereabouts. Another modern writer, Miss S. Cunningham, on the other hand, has written a somewhat imaginative and romantic story of the age in which Caxton lived. Finally, a still more recent writer, Professor H. B. Lathrop, in a paper printed in *The Library* in September, 1922, endeavours to show that Caxton has been unduly over-praised and that he was actuated in what he did by no higher motive than his own self-interest.

With the exception of William Blades, whose admiration for Caxton and his work was unbounded, none of these writers have covered the ground contained in the term "Roadmaker."

In the following pages I have endeavoured to strike out a new line. It seems to me that as a roadmaker William Caxton and his work make a strong appeal to the imagination.

To begin with he was an Englishman with an overmastering love for his country. He was a man of deep piety and strong will. His foresight and wisdom led him to grasp at once the full value of the new art of printing books as a powerful aid to knowledge and civilization, and he did not rest until he had conferred that blessing upon his countrymen. At an age when he might very well have retired to his chimney-corner, his arm-chair and the books he loved, he set himself to learn a new and difficult trade, and spent the last fifteen years of his life in selecting books of the highest literary and moral value for his English readers, in translating, editing and printing them. In his Prologues and Epilogues we get many glimpses of his character, which was certainly anything but that of a calculating and selfish tradesman.

Englishmen are justly proud of Caxton, and if in the following pages I have been able to do justice to him as a roadmaker, I shall have had my reward.

In dealing with the outlines of his life there is not much to tell that is new. A few additional references to the Caxtons of Kent have been found amongst the archives at the Public Record Office, while from the same source I have been able to add a hitherto unrecorded incident, his assignment of his property to trustees during his brief visit to England in 1453.

HENRY R. PLOMER.

WILLESDEN, 1924.

CHAPTER I

Caxton's birthplace—Description of the Weald of Kent—Character and occupations of its inhabitants—Caxtons of Kent—William Caxton's education—His apprenticeship — Robert Large of London, mercer—Caxton's life in London—Death of Robert Large—Caxton goes abroad.

IN the Prologue to the first book Caxton printed, *The Recuyell of the Historyes of Troy,* he has left it on record that he was born in the Weald of Kent, where the dialect was as "brode and rude" as in any part of England.

Unfortunately he does not say in what part of the Weald he was born, and the boundaries of that part of the "garden of England" are vague and undefined. Roughly, it extends east and west from Tunbridge Wells to Ashford, and north and south from Maidstone to the borders of

Sussex. A rich, undulating country, in olden times covered with dense forest in which boars and wolves were hunted; now dotted with picturesque towns and villages, hop gardens, orchards and marshland and retaining to this day belts of wood and coppice to remind us of its ancient wildness.

The inhabitants of the Weald were a bold, hardy and industrious people, who worked on the land, did a large trade in wool, and in the days of Edward III added cloth-weaving to their other industries, that king having invited over Flemish cloth-weavers to teach his subjects how to weave cloth, and the newcomers settled in the large towns and villages. The Kentish historian Hasted, writing in 1778, reported that in the fifteenth century the trade was "exercised by persons who possessed most of the landed property in the Weald, insomuch that almost all the ancient families of these parts, now of large estates, are sprung from ancestors who have used this staple manufacture." The "mercer" was the agent through whom the cloth was sold.

Many attempts have been made to trace the exact spot in the Weald of Kent which can claim the honour of being Caxton's birthplace. The name, like all names, was spelt in a variety of ways in olden times, Causton, Cauxton, Caxston, Caston and Caxton being some of the variants, and several families of this name can be traced in the Weald as well as in other parts of Kent in the fourteenth and fifteenth centuries. To begin with, there was a manor called "Caustons" near Hadlow, not far from Tunbridge Wells, which is on the extreme western border of the Weald; but the family who owned it had died out long before the printer's birth.

Near Cranbrooke, which lies more in the centre of the district, there is a piece of woodland, marked on the ordnance map as "Causton Wood," and Cranbrooke contained one of the largest settlements of Flemish broad-cloth weavers in the fifteenth century. It might well be the long sought for home of Caxton's parents. Not many miles away from Cranbrooke lies the pleasant town of Tenterden, which also harboured many Flemish families, and living there in 1420 was a Thomas Caxton, who witnessed the will of a fellow townsman that is preserved amongst the muniments of Westminster Abbey. Not only so, but Tenterden parish church had at that time as its vicar a certain John Mooer or More, who was a scholar and possessed an unusually fine library, of which more will be said later. He would fit the part of Caxton's tutor very well. At Sandwich, which is not in the Weald, there were several families of the name. Thus on the Plea Rolls at the Public Record Office, for Easter term, 8 Hen. VI [i.e., 1429-30], Hugh Caxston chapman and Alice his wife of Sandwich in Kent, were sued by John Warde, citizen and "mercer" of London, on a plea of debt, and this Hugh Caxston was still living there in 1453.

In researches of this kind coincidences are always cropping up to render the investigator's work more difficult, and therefore it is not surprising to find that a Richard Ward, priest, was one of our printer's executors.

We next find a Thomas Caxton taking up his freedom as a citizen of Sandwich in 1447-48, and thirty years later he is amongst the brotherhood of Bartholomew's Hospital there. This Thomas was no doubt of kin with Hugh.

Passing south once more, we find two Thomas Caxtons at Lydd, in the second half of the fifteenth century, one of whom was a priest and the other a "yeoman."

But the most remarkable family is found at Canterbury, and it is difficult to believe that these Canterbury Caxtons were not in some way related to the printer.

First we find a William Caxton, mercer, taking up his freedom as a citizen "by redemption," in 1431. [W. M. Cowper, *Freemen of Canterbury*.] Then we find in the Consistory Court there the will of a Robert Causton or Caxston, proved on the

12th July, 1573, whose principal tenement was in St. Alphege parish. This he left to his son John Caxton, also a "mercer," whose will was proved on the 28th November, 1485. John mentions a brother Thomas, "a monk," but says nothing of any William. The late J. M. Cowper was of opinion that this John was the printer's brother; but it was a pure guess, and he could never give his authority. None the less, this Canterbury family were evidently wealthy and of some position, and John used a rebus of three cakes above a tun or barrel [Cakes-Tun], which was the recognized merchants' mark of the family. If not conclusive, this evidence shows that there is no occasion to go outside the County of Kent to seek William Caxton's parents.

The date of his birth is also a matter of conjecture. Happily it offers an easier problem than his place of birth. We can get within a year or two of it, as he could scarcely have been less than fourteen years of age when he was put an apprentice with

Robert Large, mercer, of London, on 24th June, 1438, which would mean that he was born in 1424, or near it.

His education is another matter about which we should like to know more. He has left it on record that he was well educated, and learnt his English in the Weald of Kent. His parents would naturally teach him the first rudiments of speech, and they may have been sufficiently well educated themselves to do even more than that. If we could feel sure that Tenterden was his birthplace we might imagine him a pupil of Sir John More. Or again, if as appears possible, the Caxtons of Canterbury were connections, he might have been sent from his Wealden home to finish his education at the school attached to Christchurch monastery, which was situated in St. Alphege parish where John Caxton lived. In that case it would be easy to imagine among his schoolmates William Pratt, who was born in Canterbury and who we know became his life-long friend.

One thing at least shapes itself amidst the mists of uncertainty that shroud Caxton's early life. His parents, whoever they were, must have been fairly well-to-do, otherwise they could hardly have obtained entry for him into the Mercers' Company, which was the richest, most exclusive and most powerful of all the London Guilds in the fifteenth century. They were also, we feel sure, God-fearing people, who instilled into their son that piety that shows itself throughout all his writings, and taught him to do his duty in whatever situation he might find himself.

On the 24th June, 1438, Caxton was entered in the books of the Mercers' Company as one of Robert Large's apprentices. This again strengthens the belief that his parents were of some standing, for Robert Large was one of the most influential men of the Mercers' Company, and a prominent figure in the life of the City of London. In 1427 he was Warden of his Company. Again in 1430 he was elected a Sheriff, and in the year 1439-40, a year after Caxton had become his apprentice, became Lord Mayor, the highest honour the citizens could confer on him. He lived in the Old Jewry, and had a family of four sons and two daughters.

It is difficult at this distance of time to get a clear conception of the social life of the fifteenth century. It was a rougher, and as Caxton would have termed it, a "ruder" age than ours. In such matters as food, the appointments of the table, the furniture of the rooms, the sleeping accommodation and other domestic arrangements, there was much that could only be called primitive and uncomfortable. But in the households of the well-to-do, in which class we may certainly place Robert Large, we can well believe that there was a certain measure of refinement. The walls were hung with tapestries or decorated with arms and armour. The furniture was solid and substantial, and though master and servants dined together, each had his appointed place, according to his rank, and was expected to behave with decorum. The ladies had their own apartments and their several household duties and amusements, while the apprentices who were numbered amongst the servants were expected to rise early, to work industriously, and to serve their master and mistress faithfully. On the other hand, if the apprentice found himself harshly treated or ill-fed, he could carry his complaints to the Warden of the Company, who, if he was satisfied that the statements were true, could transfer him to another master.

There is no reason to suppose that the relations between Robert Large and William Caxton were other than of the most cordial nature. From his subsequent history it is clear that the young apprentice took up his duties with the full intention of working hard and learning his business, and while no doubt his character was formed largely by his parents before he came to London, we may be equally sure that as a member of the household of Robert Large he was taught the principles of piety, thrift and industry.

There was plenty of temptation in the London of the fifteenth century for the idle or dissolute apprentice; but it had no attraction for young Caxton, whose tastes were, if we may judge by his riper years, of a grave and studious nature. No account of this period of his life has been preserved, but supposing him to have been a young man of normal health and temperament, he not only took his share in the sports of his fellows—an occasional game of football in Cheapside or a match at archery in Moorfields—but also showed a lively interest in the political and social events of his time. The citizens of London had plenty to talk about during the years of Caxton's residence under Large's roof. England and France were at war, and it was going badly for England. Men shook their heads and said it would go worse yet unless things were handled better.

The rivalry between the houses of York and Lancaster kept men's minds on the rack and must have been a daily topic of conversation amongst all classes, particularly when some incident like the penance of Eleanor Chobham, Duchess of Gloucester, brought it directly to their notice. This unfortunate lady, accused of sorcery by her enemies, had been condemned to walk barefooted through the streets of the city, from the waterside to St. Paul's, with a white sheet round her and carrying a taper. As an escort, and in order to heighten her shame, the mayor, sheriff and guilds of London, in their robes, were ordered to be present, and following them we may be sure was a crowd of ragged and dirty children from all the alleys and slums with which the old city abounded. Caxton might easily have been a witness of this piteous sight, which must have roused mingled feelings of anger and sympathy in the hearts of the onlookers.

Religious troubles and the spread of Lollardism was another matter that filled the minds of the people of England at that time, and was brought home to the citizens of London by the burning on Tower Hill, in 1439, of Sir Richard Wiche, Vicar of Deptford, which, if he did not see, Caxton doubtless heard described from the lips of some who were present.

Bad harvests, bad weather and bad trade, starvation amongst the poorer classes throughout the country, formed daily items of news that went the round of the town. To Large and his household the best news was the conclusion of peace between England and Flanders in 1439. The wool trade had suffered badly from the short-sighted policy of the statesmen of the two countries, and a return to saner methods must have been welcomed by the mercers.

Robert Large did not live to see the results of the new policy. His death on the 24th April, 1441, led to a momentous change in Caxton's life. He had served but three years of his apprenticeship, and he was not released from serving out his time by the death of his master. In such cases the transfer of the apprentice to another master followed as a matter of course. Robert Large left no instructions in his will as to

Caxton's future; but he left him a bequest of twenty marks, an equivalent of £13 6s. 8d., or about £150 as reckoned by present-day standards.

All we know beyond this is that before the end of the year 1441, William Caxton had left England.

CHAPTER II

Caxton arrives in Bruges—His business abilities—Visits England in 1453—Returns to Bruges and becomes Governor of English Nation—Glimpses of his life abroad—His love of books—Translates a Flemish and French phrase-book—Louis de Bruges and his library—The new art of printing brought to Ghent where Caxton may have seen it.

WHEN we next meet with William Caxton he is a merchant of some importance in the city of Bruges, then a famous seaport on the coast of Flanders. It is not absolutely certain that he went there direct from England. All we know is that writing in 1471 he said, that he had "contynued by the space of xxx yere, for the most parte in the contres of Braband, Flandres, Holand, and Zeland." At the same time all the probabilities point to Bruges as the place. Not only was it the great emporium of the cloth and woollen trades in the fifteenth century, but it was also the headquarters of the Mercers' Company in Europe. Nor must it be forgotten that Caxton was still an apprentice. We do not know the name of his new master, but it seems very likely that he was on the point of setting out for Bruges on business, and took Caxton with him.

Caxton has left us no record of the impressions produced on his mind by the new surroundings in which he found himself; but we cannot doubt that they must have been powerful and lasting. He was then about twenty-one—the age to be impressionable. He was, we may be sure, a thoughtful and observant man, and from the moment that the towers and wharves of Bruges came into sight he saw much to fill him with wonder and delight, and while his first impressions of Flanders and its people were probably modified as he became better acquainted with its character and political history, those first impressions were never altogether obliterated.

When in the year 1369 Philip the Hardy,

Duke of Burgundy, was affianced to Margaret, the daughter of Earl Louis de Male, it is said that he hastened with joy to meet this young princess, who was bringing to him as a "dot" the County of Flanders, "the noblest, the richest and the greatest in Christendom."[1]

One of the staple industries of that rich province was the weaving of cloth, a trade which had its outlet and inlet through the port of Bruges, which was situated on a small tributary of the Scheldt, called the Zwin. In Caxton's time this river was fast silting up, but was still navigable by the small vessels of those days, which drew very little water; although by the end of the century Bruges, like Rye, Winchelsea and Pevensey on this side, had become practically an inland town, relying chiefly on its canals. In 1441 it was still flourishing, and so great was the trade carried on with England that anything that threatened the rupture of diplomatic relations between the two

[1] M. Kervyn, *Histoire de Flandre*, Tome iii, p. 407.

countries seriously affected the finances of Bruges.[1]

It was without doubt the most opulent city in Northern Europe, visited by merchants and the nobility from all the surrounding countries, and for more than two centuries it had been known as a centre of artistic life and political freedom.

Accustomed as he was to the narrow streets and gabled houses of the City of London, and to the busy life of the Thames, Caxton's first glimpse of Bruges—the fleet of ships lying in the river or beside the quays, the piles of merchandise, furs from Russia, metal from Poland and Hungary, wool, cheese and timber from Great Britain, figs from Grenada and wines from the Rhineland;[2] the unaccustomed dress and speech of those amongst whom he found himself on landing must have set his pulses quickening and filled him with a desire to know more of these people. As the months went by and

[1] L. G. Van Scœren, *Inventaire des Chartes,* Tome iv, p. 423.

[2] Weale, *Bruges et ses Environs*, p. 7.

he became more at home in this strange land, we may readily assume that its buildings, the great hall with its noble belfry in the market place, the Hôtel de Ville, the Cathedral and other churches with their paintings and sculpture, were a source of endless delight to him.

Nor was this all; the inhabitants of Bruges were renowned for the artistic way in which they decorated their streets on all festive occasions, and it was, most probably, the splendid tournaments which he saw whilst he was there that led him in after years to lament the decay of chivalry in England.

For the next thirty years Caxton's leisure was snatched from a life of hard and constant work as a merchant. That he was a keen, hard-headed, conscientious and clever man of business, such scanty glimpses as we get of him fully bear out.

His apprenticeship came to an end somewhere about the year 1445; although being resident abroad, no record of his admission to the Freedom of the Mercers' Company is to be found in their books. Exactly what happened to him after that is also a matter of surmise, whether he joined in partnership with some other "mercer" or traded on his own account. This at least becomes clear, that his business abilities were recognized by the great body of merchants amongst whom he moved, and that by the year 1450 he was in a position to become surety for one of them, in a sum of £110, or nearly £1,500 as reckoned in money of the present day. The story as recorded in the archives of the city of Bruges relates how Caxton and a brother mercer, John Selle, were sued before the authorities of the city by a certain William Craes on a plea of debt. The plaintiff deposed that a merchant named John Granton owed him the sum in question, and that John Selle and William Caxton had become sureties for Granton, who had left the country without paying his debt, whereupon, as he was entitled to do, he had caused the sureties to be arrested. The defendants admitted their liability, but pleaded that John

Granton's absence was only temporary, that he was very rich and had no intention of defrauding the plaintiff, who should wait and look to him for payment. But the judges found in favour of William Craes, and ordered the defendants to find security for the amount, at the same time stipulating that if John Granton paid the debt the complainant was to pay them as a fine double the amount claimed.

In 1453 William Caxton returned to England on a brief visit, and in company with two other "mercers" was admitted to the Livery of the Company. At the same time he made an assignment of all his property both real and personal, in England and "beyond the seas," to Robert Cosyn, citizen and "mercer" of London, and John Rede of the same city, and their heirs for ever. No reason is stated in the document for this assignment, which was duly entered on the Close Rolls and dated the 11th of December, 1453.[1]

[1] P.R.O. Close Roll 304, m. 25.

The most reasonable explanation of this act on Caxton's part seems to be that there was still trouble with William Craes, and the assignment, which was purely formal, was to protect his property from seizure. Had it been a marriage settlement we should have expected it to be worded in a different way, and to have made some reference to his wife.

In the same year the Mercers' books record that William Caxton, Richard Burgh, Thomas Bryce and William Pratt were fined for not attending upon Geffrey Fielding, mercer, when he was elected Mayor of the City of London. As the annual election of the Mayor took place in November, it would seem that Caxton was in England for some months. On his return to Bruges he devoted himself to business, and steadily rose to an important position in the counsels of the great trading guild known as the Company of Merchant Adventurers, which, while numbering amongst its members grocers, drapers, and fishmongers, was chiefly composed of members of the Company of Mercers, and had its headquarters in London at the Mercers' Hall.

Several charters had been granted by English kings to this powerful body, who took upon themselves to safeguard the rights of all English merchants trading in foreign parts, and on the accession of Edward IV an Act had been passed specially confirming all grants made to the Wardens of the Company of Mercers.

Caxton must have had an anxious time for the next ten or twelve years.

Philip the Good, who was then Duke of Burgundy, was an arrogant and passionate man. He knew no other right than force, and no other rule than his own will. The citizens of Bruges had no cause to love him, for he had encroached upon their ancient liberties and compelled them to sue for his pardon on their knees. Nor was he by any means a friend of England. He had sent his troops to take part in the siege of Calais. and in 1464 had issued a decree forbidding the importation of English cloth into his dominions, and he showed no inclination to renew the treaty of trade between the two countries which had been in force for many years, but was expiring very shortly.

As Governor of the English Nation at Bruges, to which office William Caxton had been appointed before June, 1463, he took a leading part in the negotiations that were carried on for the renewal of the treaty, and on the 24th October, 1464, King Edward IV issued a commission to Sir Richard Whetehill, afterwards Governor of Calais, and William Caxton, mercer, to negotiate with the Duke of Burgundy. These negotiations came to nothing, and the Mercers' Company thereupon wrote to Caxton advising him to consult with the representatives of the Company in Bruges as to what further steps were to be taken; while at the same time the Earl of Warwick wrote to him, calling upon him to forbid trading by English merchants with the subjects of the Duke of Burgundy, so that

Caxton's hands were full of business both private and public, his mind was occupied with weighty affairs, and much of his time was spent in travelling from place to place, even as far as Holland. He has left us two interesting glimpses of his life at this time in the pages of the *Golden Legend.* Under the heading "David" occurs this passage:

"For as I ones was by yonde the see ryding in the companye of a noble knyght named Sir John Capons, and was also doctour in bothe lawes and was born in Malyorke . . . and that tyme Counceyllour vnto the duc of Bourgonye [Burgundy] Charloys [Charles] it happened we comened [communed] of the hystorye of David, and this said noble man told me that he had redde that David dyde this penaunce. . . . Thus this noble man told me, ryding by-twene the toun of Gaunt [Ghent] in Flaunders and the toun of Bruxelles [Brussels] in Braband."

Again in the same work, when writing the life of St. Austin and the miracles performed by that Saint, he speaks of one he had seen portrayed over the altar of the church of the Black Friars in Antwerp.

But how did he spend such leisure time as he could get from his duties? Some of it we may well believe was set aside for his devotions, for Caxton was a good Catholic and a deeply religious man. He was also, we know, keen on sports, especially tournaments. Above all he was a book lover. It is not feasible that this love of acquiring books and of reading was only a growth of his later life. As an educated man he had probably been attracted to books from his boyhood, and we may readily believe that much of his leisure time was spent in reading and book-hunting. He had, moreover, unique opportunities for finding out what books were in circulation and for buying such as he fancied. Indeed, we know that this was so. At some time or another, possibly soon after his arrival at Bruges, he secured a little book of French and Flemish phrases, no doubt with the object of making himself more familiar with both those languages. The book may have been the one which was reprinted in 1875 by Monsieur Michelant of Paris, under the title of *Le Livres des Mestiers,* said to have been drawn up by a schoolmaster of Bruges in the fourteenth century: or it may have been a variant of that. Caxton must have found it useful to him in his travels; but what he wanted was not only the equivalent of the French phrases in Flemish, but also the French phrases in English, and accordingly, possibly as a recreation and in his spare time, he translated the French sentences into English, at the same time adding some phrases which he thought might be of value or interest to his countrymen. That these additional passages, which are not found in any French or Flemish copy, were written by Caxton, there is not a shadow of doubt. The long and interesting passages in which the buying of cloth is described, the many references to English money and its equivalents, the addition of London, York, Bristol and Bath to the list of places famous for their cloth, and of Sturbridge, Salisbury and St. Bartholomew's to the lists of fairs, and the mention of the "procession of Westminster," stamp these additions as the work of an Englishman, while the many references to Bruges, its streets and buildings, show that the translator was resident at that time in the city. Another touch, which could clearly have come from no other hand than Caxton's, is the altered version of the description of a bookseller's shop. In *Le Livres de Mestiers* this consists of seven lines, those printed in italics. The English version is as follows:

> *George the booke sellar*
> *Hath moo bookes*
> *Than all they of the toune.*
> He byeth them all
> Suche as they ben,
> Be they stolen or enprinted[1]

[1] Mr. H. Bradley, the editor of the reprint, thinks that the word should read "enpruntes," i.e., borrowed, and he may be right; but printing was established on the Continent when this translation was made.

Or otherwyse pourchaced
He hath doctrinals, catons,
Oures of our lady
Donettis, partis, accidents
Sawters well illumined
Bounden with clasps of silver
Bookes of physike
Seven salmes, kalenders
Ynke and perchymen,
Pennes of swannes
Pennes of ghees
Good portoses,
Which ben worth good money.

Moreover, as "Governor of the English Nation," Caxton came in contact with men of the highest rank, and was no doubt frequently a guest in their houses.

The most renowned of the citizens of Bruges in Caxton's time, by reason of his prowess, his position as commander-in-chief of the garrison, and his great wealth, was Louis de Bruges of the Gruthuyse. He was also cup-bearer to the Duke of Burgundy, and in consequence of his friendly attitude to England was created Earl of Winchester. Caxton could hardly have lived in Bruges for thirty years without coming in contact with him. There was at least one bond of sympathy between them. Louis de Bruges had for some years been forming a library. Not only did he acquire rare and valuable manuscripts by purchase; but he employed the best transcribers and illuminators in Bruges to make copies of famous books and to adorn them with his arms and those of his family, and with exquisite miniatures, and amongst those whom he employed in this way was Colard Mansion, with whom Caxton was afterwards associated as a printer. These books he had bound in the most costly and sumptuous way in velvet and satin, with precious stones and clasps and bosses of silver-gilt.

Although the bulk of Louis de Bruges's library was not acquired until after Caxton's residence there came to an end, he probably saw some of the books in it. The library was particularly rich in romances and poetry, and amongst these was a fine copy of *Le Recueil des Histoire Troyennes*. There were, however, several copies of Raoul le Fevre's work in existence, and it can hardly be supposed that it was the one in Louis de Bruges's library that Caxton afterwards translated. Amongst other manuscripts that he might have seen there were *Les Livres des Quatre Dames, Le Roman de Sept Sages, Le Roman du Lancelot du Lac* and *Le Romant de Tristant et d'Yseult.*

From what Caxton tells us himself, it is quite evident that he was more familiar with French manuscripts than with either Flemish, German or Italian, and it is quite possible, and in no way to his detriment, that his acquaintance with English books was limited to a stray volume or two shown to him by some visitor to Bruges, or some merchant who had been commissioned to procure it.

So again we may readily believe, that in the course of his journeys from place to place, he had met with some of the early printed books. The earliest block book, the *Biblia Pauperum*, is assigned to the year

1450, and the forty-two line *Bible,* the joint work of Gutenberg and Fust at Mentz, was completed in 1456, and the firm of Fust and Schoeffer continued to be the only printers in Europe until the sack of Mentz in 1462 drove their workmen into all parts of the Continent; so that long before 1471, Caxton, we may be sure, was not only familiar with books in print but had very likely seen a printing press at work at Ghent or elsewhere. He at once realized its immense value as an instrument towards the spread of learning, and clearly foresaw the revolution it was going to make in the political and social history of the world. Like Captain Cuttle, he "made a note of it," and perhaps at the same time registered a vow that, with God's help, there should one day be a printing press in England.

CHAPTER III

Caxton reads the *Recueil des Histoires de Troyes*—His first attempt to translate it a failure—Arrival of Margaret, sister to King Edward IV, and her marriage to Charles, Duke of Burgundy — Her friendship for Caxton encourages him to continue his translation of the *Recueil*—Caxton learns to print at Cologne—Returns to Bruges and sets up as a printer with Colard Mansion—Prints his translation of the *Recueil* and other books — Returns to England.

MEANWHILE events were moving fast in Flanders. Philip the Good died on June 15th, 1467, and his son Charles became Duke of Burgundy. It was about this time that Caxton began reading the French manuscript by Raoul le Fevre, *Le Recueil des Histoires de Troyes*. The book gripped him. He tells us that he had "great pleasyr and delyte" in reading it, both on account of its novelty and the grace of the language. The work had only been written three years before, and as he had never seen or heard of an English translation, and fired by enthusiasm, he there and then took pen and ink and started to make a translation of the volume he was reading into English. But he found the task harder than he had anticipated, and after he had written four or five quires he became disheartened and disgusted with his work. Fortunately he did not tear up what he had done, but he laid the sheets aside, and for the time gave up the attempt and thought no more of the matter for two years.

In the following year (1468) ambassadors were sent from England to propose to Charles a marriage with Margaret, the sister of King Edward IV. The matter was speedily and satisfactorily arranged, and the marriage was celebrated at Bruges with great splendour and much rejoicing. Margaret was attended by a large retinue of nobles from the English Court, and amid the pealing of bells and the acclamation of the people the newly married couple were escorted through the gaily decorated streets by a cavalcade of knights in armour, representative of the highest families in both kingdoms. Feasts and tournaments followed, and no doubt Caxton, as "Governor of the English Nation," was amongst those presented to Margaret and her husband, and then met the future Earl Rivers, the Duke of Arundel and many of those who gave him such ready help and loyal support in days to come.

In the following year Caxton left Bruges and apparently entered the service of the Duchess of Burgundy. In order to do so he resigned his position as "Governor of the English Nation," and his reasons for making this change in his life have given rise to much speculation.

But the explanation appears to be a very natural and simple one. Like Caxton, when he first came to Bruges, Margaret was a stranger in a strange land. She would naturally want to surround herself with as many of her own nationality as she could.

She was, moreover, a highly educated woman and a lover of books, and by her marriage to the Duke of Burgundy she had come into possession of the finest library in Europe. It was books, probably more than anything else, that cemented her friendship with Caxton. He, for his part, no doubt, felt that he had done his share of hard work, and welcomed the prospect of greater leisure under a lady who was not only his country-woman, but was also a book-lover. Does it not seem more than likely that the post offered to him by the Duchess was that of secretary and librarian, rather than merely as most writers have supposed, a buyer of wool for her and her husband?

Whatever his position was, "on a time it fortuned," to use his own words, that the Duchess sent for Caxton "to speke wyth her good grace of dyuerce maters." This is provokingly vague. Where was Margaret living at that time? When did this interview take place, and what were the diverse matters that she wanted his advice about?

The Dukes of Burgundy had a palace in Bruges, which contained a library of nearly 2,000 volumes. It may have been there, or possibly in Ghent, early in 1470, on the occasion of the investiture of the Duke of Burgundy with the Order of the Garter.

As regards the "dyuerce maters," we believe that books and literature were the chief topics discussed between them; because it is most improbable that had the conversation been about other matters, Caxton would have volunteered the information that he had some two years before attempted to translate the *Recueil* into English.

There was no hesitancy on the part of the young Duchess on hearing this surprising news; no indifference or half-hearted words of congratulation; her face aglow with delight, she commanded "him to show her at once what he had done."

Although it only occupies a sentence or two in Caxton's Prologue, the events described were probably spread over several days or weeks. In the first place Caxton, we infer, had not got those five or six quires in his pocket. The subject had merely cropped up casually in the course of a general conversation about books, so that if he was in Ghent at the time, he had to return to Bruges in order to find these sheets which he had put aside. When he did show them to her, there was no discouragement to be feared from his mistress. She was in every way helpful, as one who understood.

Caxton's own words are best here: "and whan she had seen hem, anone she fonde defaute in myn Englisshe whiche she coma[n]ded me to amende a[n]d more ouer comanded me straytly to contynue and make an ende of the resydue than not translated, whos dredfull com[m]a[n]dement y durst in no wyse disobey becase y am a serva[n]t unto her sayd grace and resseiue of her yerly fee and other many goode and grete benefets, and also hope many moo to resseyve of her highnes, but forthwith wente and labouryde in the said translacion aftyr my simple and poor conning also nygh as I can followyng myn auctour," etc., etc.

We may substitute for the words "commandment" and "dreadful commandment" the words "encouragement" and "goodwill"; Margaret's "dreadful commandment" probably amounted to no more than a "desire" that he should continue what he had begun, and to an expression that it would greatly please her, and that she would help him to amend his "rude" English. On the other hand, Caxton's statement that he was afraid to disobey her for fear of losing his post was only a cloak to hide his pleasure at her encouraging words. She applied the spur that quickened him to work that he loved: work that was to bring in its train mighty results.

We know that he had begun the translation of the *Recueil* at Bruges, he now continued it at Ghent, and finished it in Cologne in the following year.

A recent discovery made by Lieutenant-Colonel J. C. Birch in the register of aliens at Cologne,[1] proves that Caxton arrived in Cologne in July, 1471, and remained there until after Midsummer, 1472. We may suppose that he was there with the knowledge and consent of the Duchess of Burgundy. Did he go there for the express purpose of learning the art of printing? He had doubtless frequently discussed the new art and its possibilities with her, and he had evidently undertaken, if she would give her consent, to defray the expenses out of his own pocket. He had already promised copies of the *Recuyel of the Historyes of Troy* to many noblemen and friends, and he gives the following reasons for the step he had taken:

"And for as moche as in the wrytyng of the same my penne is worn, myn hand wery and not stedfast, myn eyen dimed with ouermoche lokyng on the whit paper, and my corage not so prone and redy to laboure

[1] *Transactions of the Bibliographical Society*, June, 1923, p. 50.

as hit hath been, and that age crepeth on me dayly and feebleth all the bodye, and also be cause I have promysed to dyuerce gentilmen and to my frendes to addresse to hem as hastely as I myght this sayd book. Therefore I have practysed and lerned at my grete charge and dispense to ordeyne this said book in printe after the maner and forme as ye may here see."

The discovery made by Lieutenant-Colonel Birch sets at rest the vexed question as to where Caxton learnt the art of printing. In the Bartholomæus *De Proprietatibus Rerum*, printed by Wynkyn de Worde about 1495, the printer inserted at the end the following lines:

> And also of your charyte call to remembraunce
> The soule of William Caxton, the fyrste prynter of this boke
> In Laten tongue at Coleyn hymself to avaunce
> That every well disposyd man may thereon loke

This was a spontaneous testimonial to his late master, and no one had more authority to speak on the subject than the man who had worked with him ever since he had been in England. Moreover, Mr. E. Gordon Duff, the greatest of modern authorities on all that concerns the art of printing in England, identified the Latin edition mentioned in the above lines as having been printed or partly printed by Caxton at Cologne, with the edition by a printer in that city, known as the printer of a work called *Flores Augustini.*[1]

But William Blades, Caxton's biographer, held that it was with Colard Mansion that he learnt to print, his reasons being that Caxton's early work was inferior to that of the Cologne printers of that date; but it has been conclusively proved that there were printers of varying degrees of skill there, as indeed might be expected, seeing that the art was still young. All that Caxton wanted to learn at Cologne was the probable cost of setting up a printing office and the elementary work of a printer, and both he

[1] Library, 4th Series, June, 1923, pp. 50-52.

achieved, the second by helping to print the Latin edition of *De Proprietatibus*.

This done he returned to Bruges, possibly towards the end of 1472, and presented the finished translation of the *Recuyel of the Histories of Troy* to his mistress. What a meeting that must have been! We seem to hear Margaret's words of praise and delight as she received the volume from the hands of Caxton, and which probably in his opinion constituted the best "reward" she could give him, though doubtless they were accompanied with "largesse" of a more substantial kind.

It may be asked, why did not Caxton, when he was working in a printing house in Cologne, print the *Recuyel* there? The answer may be that, before leaving Bruges, he had come to some arrangement with Colard Mansion, and perhaps with the Duke and Duchess of Burgundy and Louis de Bruges, to start a printing press there on his return, and it would seem as if it was Caxton who taught Mansion the art of printing, rather than, as William Blades supposed, the other way about. Van Praet, in his *Recherches sur Louis de Bruges* (p. 12), states that it was that nobleman who helped Mansion to set up his press; but he ignores Caxton's share in the business, which was, no doubt, considerable.

The next eighteen months appear to have been occupied by Caxton and Mansion in the necessary preparations. By this time the art had spread to many other towns, including Louvain, where a certain John Veldener, a man of education and capital, was carrying on not only the trade of a printer but also that of a type-founder, and Mr. E. Gordon Duff points out that in 1475 Veldener "made use of a type in many respects identical with one used by Caxton. In body they are precisely the same, and in most of the letters they are to all appearances identical; and the fact of their making their appearance about the same time in the *Lectura super Institutionibus* of Angelus de Aretio, printed at Louvain by Veldener, and in the *Quatres Derrenieres Choses*, printed at Bruges by Caxton, would certainly appear to point to some connection between the two printers."[1] This type, known as Caxton's No. 1, was a bold and handsome letter, modelled on the manuscript hand of Colard Mansion, who, as we have already seen, was employed by Louis de Bruges to make copies of notable books for his library, and whose absence from Bruges during the year 1473 was due perhaps to a visit to Louvain for the purpose of obtaining type.

The first book printed in the English language was Caxton's translation of the *Recuyell of the Historyes of Troye,* and it was printed at the press of Caxton and Colard Mansion at Bruges in the course of the year 1474. It was a small folio of 352 leaves, which showed off the type to the best effect, while the use of red ink in some places still further added to its good appearance.

The first part of Caxton's dream was

[1] E. G. Duff, *William Caxton*, Caxton Club, Chicago, 1905, p. 27.

realized. He had printed a book in English for the delight of his countrymen, and at the same time had avoided the painful task of multiplying copies by hand, and we may be sure that the first to congratulate him on his success and spur him on to further efforts was the young Duchess of Burgundy.

For the next two years Colard Mansion and William Caxton worked in partnership, and amongst the books they produced in the year 1476 were two that for different reasons have an important bearing on this history. Caxton had been reading a French translation of J. de Cessolis, *Liber de Ludo Scachorum*, in which Life was likened to a game of chess. Its high moral and intellectual tone appealed to Caxton, and, as usual, his first thought was to translate it into English for the benefit and instruction of his countrymen, under the title of the *Game and Play of the Chess Moralized,* and this, the second book printed in English, he dedicated to the king's brother, the Duke of Clarence.

As showing how little weight is to be attached to the foolish theory that Caxton was a man of no originality, and that he did not in any way influence the public taste in reading, here we find him translating for the second time a book that he thought Englishmen would like to have in their own language.

No one asked him to do it, and no one paid him for doing it. In the Prologue he speaks of himself as being "unknown" to the Royal personage to whom he dedicates it. This statement was an addition to and *not* copied from De Vignay's Prologue to Prince John of France.

The other book of the year 1476, the *Quatres Derrenieres Choses,* was that in which Caxton tried a new fount of type, that known as type 2. He now felt himself in a position to carry out his long cherished hope of one day setting up a printing-press in his native country. He had spent thirty-five years of his life on the Continent. He had seen the printing office in Bruges firmly established, and felt that Colard Mansion could carry on alone. So with this new type and other necessary material, Caxton bade farewell to Flanders and returned to England.

We may be sure that the Duchess of Burgundy was loth to lose his services and his companionship, for he was a wise counsellor and a God-fearing man; but she shared with him the desire to see the benefits that would assuredly follow the introduction of printing, conferred upon her own land, and we can almost hear her wishing him "God-speed" and success in his venture.

CHAPTER IV

State of learning in England in the fifteenth century—Number of those able to read—Evidence of wills—Influence of Universities—The literature Caxton found to print—Gower, Chaucer and Lydgate.

WHAT was the nature of the soil in which William Caxton proposed to sow the seed of universal knowledge by means of the printing-press? In other words, who were the readers he hoped to reach, and what books were there in England for him to print?

Only the nucleus of a Royal library was then in being; but both King Edward IV and King Henry VII were lovers of books, and were amongst those who encouraged Caxton in his venture.

Amongst the ladies of the Royal household who were interested in his work, we have already met with Margaret, Duchess of Burgundy, sister of King Edward IV.

There was also Queen Elizabeth and Margaret, Duchess of Beaufort, and others whose names have not come down to us. Many of the nobility were educated men and book-collectors, and these again, notably Earl Rivers, the Earl of Arundel, the Earl of Oxford and the Earl of Worcester, not only welcomed the advent of Caxton's press, but brought him books out of their libraries to print. But the largest class of educated persons in England at that time were the clergy, who not only filled the highest offices of state, but were the lawyers and school-masters as well as the transcribers and illuminators of manuscripts.

It is in the wills of archbishops, bishops, deans, priests and clerks, that mention of books is chiefly found. Archbishop John de Stretforde, Archbishop of Canterbury, who died in 1348, left all his service books to the Chapel of St. Thomas of Stratford, and other books amongst his friends. Richard Aungervyle, Bishop of Durham, better known as Richard de Bury, bequeathed his library, which was said to be the largest in England, to Oxford University. John Grandison, Bishop of Exeter, who died in 1369, Walter Skirlaw, Bishop of Durham (1406), Walter Medeford, Dean of Wells (1421), all left large bequests of books, chiefly theological. Amongst the books possessed by John Newton, Treasurer of York Cathedral, whose will was proved in 1414, were the works of Alcuin, the writings of John Hovedon, author of various Latin poems, and those of Richard Rolle of Hampole, and Walter Hilton, the author of the *Scala Perfectionis*.

John Mooer, or More, who died in 1489, was Vicar of Tenterden, in the Weald of Kent, Caxton's homeland. To the church in which he had officiated he left a *Graduale*, the devotional work known as *Pupilla Oculi*, and a gloss upon the Gospels; to Christ-church, Canterbury, *A Concordance of the Bible*, and other theological works; to Canterbury College in Oxford the works of Petrus Lombardus, better known as The

Master of Sentences; to Eton College *The Epistles of Augustine,* and several other books of a like character; to the Monastery of St. Augustine in Canterbury, to Magdalen College, Oxford, and to the colleges of Wye and Ashford in Kent, various theological books. Amongst the friends to whom he bequeathed books were William Wyrsham of the house of St. Thomas of Acres, in London; Sir John Gilford, knight; Thomas Copland, Rector of Biddenden, in Kent; Richard Prutt, Rector of Sandhurst; and Robert Shefeld, Rector of Chartham. To a certain John Carlesse he bequeathed a copy of *The Æneids of Virgil*, to another friend Tully's *De Officiis*, and to the famous Greek scholar, Thomas Linacre, a sum of ten pounds and various printed books.

This, be it remembered, was the library of a single parish priest, perhaps a rich man, but there were hundreds of others like him in various parts of the country, and even the poorest of these priests possessed some kind of service book, which at his death he left to his parish church.

Nor must it be assumed from the absence of any mention of books in a man's will that he could not read, and possessed none. Take as an example the will of Caxton's great friend, William Pratt, who died in 1486. It makes no mention of any books, yet we know that he was a lover of books, that he owned some, and had lent one of them to the printer to be translated and printed. In many cases the books were probably included in the residue of a testator's property, being too few in number and perhaps too unimportant to be specially mentioned.

Passing from libraries of individuals to those of institutions, all the large monastic establishments throughout the kingdom possessed libraries of considerable size. Bury St. Edmunds is said to have possessed 2,000 books, Titchfield Abbey we are told owned over 1,000, and the monasteries of York and Durham each held a large store of books. But there is no need to go further than Caxton's own county of Kent to see how rich and varied were the collections of literature to be found in monastic buildings.

The Abbey Church of St. Augustine in Canterbury, in the fifteenth century, had a library that contained about 1,900 volumes, with a large section devoted to works on history, an equally large section filled with classical authors, and other sections in which works on arithmetic, geometry and kindred sciences were well represented, and which also possessed the romances of *Guy of Warwick, The Knight of the Swan, Lancelot du Lac, The Story of the Graal,* and *The Four Sons of Aymon.*

The monastic library of Christchurch, Canterbury, was about the same size as that of its neighbour. Prior Eastry's catalogue, drawn up before 1331, enumerated 1,850 volumes, and that number must have been considerably increased before the end of the fifteenth century.

On the other hand, a considerable number of the books had been transferred to Oxford on the foundation of Canterbury College, so that probably the number of volumes on the shelves remained much about the same as when Eastry made his catalogue. Theology and canon law filled most of the presses; but the Christchurch library was rich in history and classical literature, and though it contained few books by English authors, and romances may be looked for in vain in the catalogue, the British Museum has one of the Canterbury volumes, in which amongst other writings is a version of the romance *Dares Phrygius*. [Cottonian Vespasian Bxxv. ff. 96^{b}-117.]

In addition to these two large collections of books in Canterbury, there was a smaller library in Dover Priory consisting of about 450 books, of which one section included chronicles and romances and another poetry. Amongst the romances were the two famous French works, *Le Romaunt de la Rose* and *Le Romaunt du Roy Charlemagne*, and in poetry were the writings of Ovid, Terence and Juvenal.

Next to the monastic establishments as homes of learning came the two Universities. By the commencement of the sixteenth century the number of separate foundations in Oxford and Cambridge was almost what it is to-day. Amongst the oldest and most famous colleges in Oxford were Baliol, Canterbury, Christchurch, Merton and Queens; and in Cambridge, Corpus Christi, Trinity and the University, and each and all of these possessed collections of books bequeathed to them by their founders, by the professors who taught in them and lived their lives in their precincts, as well as by pupils who had taken their degrees there or studied in them. As to the nature of the contents of these early college libraries, Dr. M. R. James, who is the greatest authority on medieval manuscripts, writes as follows:

"In all cases known to me, the books in question are in the main undistinguished by external beauty, are written evidently with a view to cheapness, and contain only the works most commonly read in the schools. There are, to be sure, exceptions; we occasionally find books written, a couple of centuries before a college was founded, in the scriptorium of some great monastery, which has sold them as duplicates or perhaps presented them to a monk studying at the University. . . . Generally speaking, however, the gifts of the medieval Fellows, and the purchases made by colleges in medieval times are strictly practical and prosaic." [*Descriptive Catalogue of the Manuscripts in the Library of Pembroke College, Cambridge,* Introduction, p. vii.]

It was not until after the dispersal of the monastic libraries on their dissolution that the Oxford and Cambridge Colleges secured the treasures of which they are now proud. Nevertheless, "practical and prosaic" as they were, these college manuscripts served as the basis of many a book that passed through the printing-press in after years.

Amongst the students and undergraduates in these colleges there were many who were not intended for the church, and who either led the lives of country squires or became merchants or took up other professions in life. They carried away with them the power of reading, and we may be quite sure that a large proportion of them bought books to read, although they may never have owned a sufficient number to be dignified with the name of a library. Caxton knew several such, and three of them, his great friends, William Pratt and Hugh Bruce, mercers, and another "worshipful merchant," whom he does not name, were amongst those who brought him books to print.

Finally there was another source from which the ranks of educated persons were recruited in those days. Every large monastic church, such as Tewkesbury Abbey and all the great cathedrals, had a choir composed of men and boys. The men were monks belonging to the establishment; but any boy in the town or city possessed of a good voice was secured for the cathedral choir, and received as part payment a free education. These again passed out into the world with sufficient knowledge to desire the possession of books.

It is often said that the number of readers in Caxton's day were few. The foregoing survey seems to point to a very much larger number of readers than is generally supposed. And this leads naturally to another consideration. How much of the road was made when Caxton took a hand in the work? In what branches of literature had Englishmen up to that time made any name?

In the field of theology, from Bede to Langland, there were a host of English writers and commentators. In particular the devotional works of such men as Brunne, Hilton, Hovedon and Rolle were so popular that they were copied, not only in the scriptoriums, but by professional scriveners in large numbers.

In that of history there was a rich collection of chronicles compiled by Englishmen, such as no other country could produce, and which were remarkable for "variety of interest, wealth of information and amplitude of range." [*Cambridge History of English Literature*, Vol. i, p. 157.] Robert of Gloucester, William of Malmesbury, Roger of Hovedon and Henry of Huntingdon were some of the writers whose work was known in many manuscripts. But there were two others who towered above them all for widely different reasons: Geoffrey of Monmouth's *Metrical Chronicle* has been called the "fountain head of Arthurian Romance," and though it was not history it was a very fascinating book. The other was Ralph Higden's *Polychronicon*, compiled by a monk of St. Werburg's, Chester, and brought down in the first instance to the year 1327, and continued by the compiler down to 1342. It was the most comprehensive and trustworthy chronicle that had ever been compiled. It was a universal history, and it continued to be extremely popular long after Caxton's death.

In the scientific world the writings of Roger Bacon, philosopher and mystic, were the most advanced in thought and speculation, and were most in demand.

It was, however, in the realm of poetry that Englishmen excelled, and the fourteenth century had produced three men whose work was destined to gain immortality and to exercise an influence upon English life, manners, speech, literature and thought, that more than anything said or done by their predecessors, has helped to make the English race what it is to-day. Those three men were Gower, Chaucer and Lydgate. The earliest in point of time was John Gower, who is believed to have been connected with the family of Sir Robert Gower, a landowner in Kent. Sir Robert died about 1349 and was buried in the church of Brabourne, near Ashford in that county, where at one time there was a brass to his memory, and the arms borne by the poet were the same as those on the brass, and other records go to prove his connection with the Gowers of Brabourne. Very little is known of his early life or education. He was a wealthy man and lived the life of a country gentleman; but he had a gift for poetry, and his most interesting work was his *Confessio Amantis*, an English poem written at the request of King Richard II and consisting of tales and meditations on love drawn from Ovid and later sources. It is believed to have been composed before 1386. He issued a revised version in 1393 in which all mention of King Richard is omitted. He was also the author of a number of love poems in Latin, French and English. In addition to the *Confessio* he wrote a Latin poem *Vox Clamantis*, dealing with Cade's rebellion, to which he added a *Chronica Triparita*, dealing with historical events down to the abdication of Richard II. In his later life Gower became blind, and spent the closing years of his life in the Priory of St. Mary Overies (now St. Saviour's, Southwark). He died in 1408, and was buried in St. Saviour's, where there is a monument to his memory. There were many manuscripts of the *Confessio Amantis* in existence in Caxton's day, but the demand was much greater than the supply.

Geoffrey Chaucer was a Londoner, the son of John Chaucer, a vintner in Thames Street. He was born about 1340, and the first heard of him is in 1357, when he was a page to Elizabeth de Burgh, wife of Lionel, Duke of Clarence. In 1359 he took part in the campaign in France and was taken prisoner. He next appears as yeoman in the King's chamber in 1367, and was granted a pension. Between 1372-73 he was on a mission in Italy, and met Boccaccio and Petrarch. After his return to England he held many lucrative offices, such as comptroller of the customs and subsidies on wool, and he was chosen to undertake several secret missions abroad, and during one of his absences he appointed John Gower one of his attorneys; but subsequently trouble arose between them. In 1386 he was elected a Knight of the Shire for Kent. In 1399 he leased a house in Westminster, where he died in 1400. Amongst Chaucer's best known poems are *The House of Fame, The Assembly of Foules, Troylus and Cressyde,* and *The Legend of Good Women;* but his largest and most delightful book was the *Canterbury Tales.*

The subject was one that appealed to all classes, rich and poor alike, for it was considered a sacred duty to go on pilgrimage, and the most popular pilgrimage in England was that to the shrine of St. Thomas à Becket at Canterbury. Nor was this surprising. Becket's murder was accompanied by all the gruesome details so dear to the morbid and the curious. Besides, the pilgrimage furnished an excuse for several days' holiday through one of England's most beautiful counties, and Chaucer, who had covered the ground, chose a pleasant time of the year, the spring, in which to set his pilgrims in motion. The whole setting was typically English, and the dress and manners of the various pilgrims were sketched in strong homely language that made a vivid appeal to the imagination. The demand for copies of the *Canterbury Tales* must have been large and continuous, but until Caxton, who loved the book, put it into print, the great majority of readers had to be content with hearing about it, and hoping that some day they might be rich enough to buy a copy.

John Lydgate was born in Suffolk at Lydgate, near Newmarket. It is possible that as a boy he was sent to the school kept by the monks in the monastery of Bury St. Edmunds. He was a high spirited lad, full of mischief, but he sobered down after his admission to the Abbey, and there are reasons for believing that he studied at one, if not both the Universities. He then appears to have gone abroad, and on his return was ordained a priest on April 7th, 1397. His gifts as a poet quickly brought him to public notice, and his knowledge of the London of his day and its citizens is quaintly and humorously shown in one of his earliest poetic efforts, *London Lack-*

penny, in which he portrays the woes of a man with an empty purse. At the request of the City of London he celebrated some of the civic ceremonies in verse. In 1412 he began his *Troy Book* at the request of the Prince of Wales, afterwards Henry V. He acted as court poet, and his patron was Humphrey, Duke of Gloucester.

On the 22nd April, 1439, he was granted a pension of ten marks from the customs of Ipswich. [Pat. Roll 17 Hen. VI, Part 1, m. 7.] Lydgate is believed to have died in 1451. Hallam describes Lydgate as "an easy versifier who served to make poetry familiar to the many." On the other hand, another of his biographers says he had little or no poetic imagination. We cannot pretend to decide between these two opposite views. The great popularity of his work, not only in his own day but also in this twentieth century, is perhaps the best warrant of his skill as a poet. His works were numerous and range themselves into many classes; but the chief of them were the

Falls of Princes, believed to have been written between 1430 and 1438; *Troy Book* mentioned above; *The Story of Thebes; The Life of Our Lady; The Court of Sapience; The Temple of Glas,* a version of Æsop; *The Horse, the Goose and the Sheep,* a moral fable.

In addition to these popular writers, there was the great field of romance, the histories of *Guy of Warwick* and *Bevis of Southampton* and such like, as well as the great Arthurian legends. Caxton bears witness that there were "large volumes and bookes, grete and plenty, and many of seynt graal, ghalehot, Launcelot, Gawayn, Perceval, Lyonel, Tristram and many others," and that they were to be found in Latin, French and English, and many other languages.

From all of which we may gather that there was no lack of books in manuscript for Caxton to print, and no lack of persons likely to become purchasers of his books when printed.

CHAPTER V

Caxton's arrival at Westminster—Position of the "Red Pale"—Caxton's motives for settling there—What his printing house looked like—His primitive methods—His first issues—The beginning of the road—First book with a date—Chaucer's *Canterbury Tales*—Number of copies to edition.

THE earliest record of William Caxton's settlement in England as a printer is an entry found in the rent-roll of John Esteney, sacrist of Westminster Abbey, for the year beginning September 29th, 1476, and ending September 28th, 1477: "De alia shopa ibidem dimisso Willelmo Caxton. X^s" (For another shop in the same let to William Caxton, 10s.). The exact date, it will be noticed, is not given, but it is generally assumed that he took possession of the premises before the end of the year 1476. This shop bore the heraldic sign of the "Red Pale," and it was situated in that part of the precincts of the Abbey known as the "Almonesrye," the place from whence alms were distributed to the poor, near the Chapel of St. Anne, and also near the alms-houses built by Lady Margaret, mother of King Henry VII, and was on the south side of the West Gate of the Close.

The description of the building as a shop and not a "house" or "tenement," seems to imply that it consisted of one or two rooms only, with a roof over them, much the same as those found on the north side of St. Paul's Cathedral at a later date, and that it contained no living rooms, in which case Caxton and his workmen must have lived elsewhere.

On this point it is worth recalling that the late Dr. Edward Scott, while in charge of the muniments at Westminster, found a document relating to the election of Abbot Islip, successor to Esteney, in which a Richard Caston (possibly a variant of Causton or Caxton) was mentioned as Master of the Novices in the Abbey between the years 1498 and 1500, who may very well have held that office or served in the Abbey twenty years earlier (*Athenæum*, June 15th, 1895). There is no evidence in support of Dr. Scott's surmise that the monk was related to the printer; but, if they knew each other, they might possibly have shared the same rooms. There was also a William Caxton buried in the Church of St. Margaret, Westminster, in 1479, and a Mawde Caxton buried there in 1490; but again, the relationship of these persons to the printer has never been proved; but these entries in the Registers of St. Margaret lend some colour to the theory that there was more than one family of the name in Westminster at the time when Caxton took possession of the "Red Pale."

The motives that led him to set up his press at Westminster rather than in the City of London have always been a fascinating subject of speculation, and although we shall never know which of the many and various solutions put forward is correct, those motives, which had such far-reaching results, will never cease to be a matter of wonder and surmise.

In the first place, there is little doubt that he had confided his plans to his friends, the Duchess of Burgundy and Earl Rivers. Nor must it be forgotten that in October, 1470, King Edward IV of England was a temporary fugitive from his throne, and was enjoying the hospitality of the Duke and Duchess of Burgundy. That Caxton was presented to him at that time, and that subsequently the Duchess told her brother of Caxton's intention to set up a press in England, is almost certain, and that the King promised him some kind of support is equally obvious. Over and over again in his Prologues and Epilogues, Caxton tells us that such and such a book had been translated and printed by him, "under the shadow of" the King's protection, "or with his protection or suffrance," or under the "umbre and shadow of the noble protection of oure moost drade soueraign," from which we may assume that one of his motives in settling at Westminster was to be near the Court, and under the King's protection. Mr. E. Gordon Duff suggests that the neighbourhood of the Abbey was a place much favoured by merchants of the Staple and dealers in wool, and that this circumstance may have influenced Caxton in making his choice, while another writer hazards the conjecture that Caxton's chief reason for settling in Westminster was that "in this powerful shelter and gracious centre of learning, he would be free from vexatious restrictions and trade jealousies." [S. Cunningham, *William Caxton*, 1917, p. 74.] There is very much to be said in support of this writer's views. There was bound to be an antagonistic feeling amongst the text writers and scriveners who formed so large a part of the Guild of Stationers, to the new art of multiplying books by machinery. They may well have thought, as they and most of the clergy did, that it was an unholy thing and savoured of the devil. Not only so, but this William Caxton was not even a member of the Guild of Stationers, and certain it is, that had he set up his press within the City of London, the Stationers would quickly have laid an information against him before the Mayor for infringing their privileges, and there were many other minor points, such as wages and the taking of apprentices, which were strictly ruled by the civic authorities. But at Westminster Caxton was outside the jurisdiction of the City, and under the shadow of the Abbey could do pretty much as he liked.

He may also have been influenced in his choice of position by the thought that, if other work failed, he could employ his press in the production of service-books. As a matter of fact, his output in this direction was small, and there is no evidence that he received any support from the Abbot, or his clergy, though it is hard to believe that they evinced no interest in the new art of multiplying books and by this means spreading the light of the Gospel. But within a stone's-throw of the "Red Pale" two men were carrying on their official duties when Caxton set up his press. One of these was Benet Burgh, Canon of the chapel of St. Stephens, and he at once grasped the importance of the new invention, and within a few months, nay, for all we know, within a few days, placed in Caxton's hands the manuscript of a translation which he had made a year or two before, of Cato's "distichs," for the instruction of the young son of the Earl of Essex.

The other was Otnel Fulle or Fuller, "master of the scholars at the Almonry," who lived in a house within the precincts which went by the name of "St. Albans," and who may or may not be identical with that mysterious printer, called by Caxton's successor Wynkyn de Worde, "sometyme scholemayster of St. Albons," who was at work between the years 1479 and 1485, and who used a fount of type that bore a remarkable likeness to one of Caxton's.

Leaving these realms of uncertainty, let

us in imagination enter the "Red Pale" and see what Caxton's printing office looked like. We can get a very fair idea of what we should see from the many illustrations and descriptions of printing offices in the fifteenth and sixteenth centuries that have come down to us, as, though some are perhaps fifty years later than Caxton's time, no change had taken place either in the printing-presses or methods of printing since the days of Gutenburg and Fust.

Naturally, the eye is first arrested by the printing-press, which occupied the centre of the floor. This was a substantial framework of timber and iron, the mechanical part being fitted with an ordinary worm-screw and lever. It was in fact just like the old cheese press in use at the beginning of the last century. The tympan, the frisket and the methods of pulling underwent very little change during the next three centuries. The work was very hard and required muscular men. On a form near to the printing-press were pots of ink and inking "balls," which were not unlike boxing-gloves tied to the end of a stick. Near one of the windows stood the compositors' cases, containing the type, punctuation marks, quadrets, etc., each letter in its own compartment, and close to these or above them was a rest to hold the manuscript. The type was placed by the compositor in a small wood or metal frame, graduated to the required length of line, and when the line was completed it was transferred to the "forme," and when a page was complete it was wedged up firmly and the forme placed in the press. Then followed the process of inking, which was done by saturating the balls with ink and beating them on the type, a dirty and clumsy process, which often resulted in some of the letters being pulled out of the forme, dropped on the floor, and reinserted by the printer anyhow and anywhere. The paper, which stood in piles ready to hand, was then placed on the forme, the lever was pulled, and the impression taken. If for any reason such as over-inking, blurred impression, defective letters or wrong composition the first pull was unsatisfactory, it was cast aside as "waste" and another "pull" taken, until a clean and correct impression was obtained. When one looks at one of Caxton's printed books it appears absolutely marvellous how he contrived to get such clean, clear and correct impressions. In many instances the ink is almost as black to-day as when it was laid on, while the even spacing of the lines and the general correctness of the compositor's work show that Caxton was most particular about the appearance of his books: but it was a slow process, and at first only one page could be printed at a time unless the office possessed more than one press.

Here and there about the room were shelves for holding books or blocks. There was also an ante-room, called the "casting-house," in which were moulds and matrices, a furnace to melt lead, and instruments in which defective type could be repaired or new type cast if necessary.

Caxton's foreman, Wynkyn de Worde,

who probably came to England with him, was at first the mechanic; he possibly doubled the parts of compositor and pressman, and there was doubtless a boy employed, who afterwards came to be known as a printer's "devil" because he got so black, who did the inking, swept the office, and ran errands. Caxton himself no doubt took a large share in the work of printing and correcting in the early days of the press, but when his workmen became more experienced he confined himself chiefly to the translation and editing of his books, for which purpose he would certainly have had a private room. Later on he took to binding his books, and this meant larger premises.

In many ways Caxton as a printer was far behind his continental brethren. He did not use signatures until he had been at work for six years. He rarely used head-lines and never used catch-words, while none of his books had any title page, and few of them have either foliation or pagination. He was also extremely sensitive in the matter of illustrations, he had very few wood-cut initial letters and only one decorative border.

No doubt these primitive methods were due partly to his want of training. He did his printing both at Bruges and Westminster as he had learned to do it in that unknown printing office in Cologne.

But apart from that Caxton had a noble conception of his duty as a printer. To him the mere mechanical process was a secondary consideration. His aim was to perpetuate such books, for preference those of English authors, or translators, as had the highest moral or literary value, and so long as the paper was strong and durable, the type clear and readable, and the press-work correct, nothing else mattered. The road he set out to make was none other than to educate and brighten the lives of his countrymen, by circulating hundreds of copies of the best literature at a low price where only half a dozen had been obtainable before, and those only by the rich.

The type that he brought with him from

Bruges was, like that with which he had printed the *Recuyell,* cut and cast by John Veldener of Louvain. This type 2, like its predecessors, was a copy of the manuscript hand seen in written books of the period; but it showed a great advance in the art of letter-cutting and artistic treatment. In all respects it was a much handsomer and more picturesque fount than its simple and unadorned brother type 1. The letters are better formed, better cast, and better finished. The sweeping curves of the lower case letters "v," "w" and "y" give to the printed page a bolder and more graceful look, and the only link with the older fount was the retention of the pump-handle filial to the letters "d" and "g" when used at the end of a word. Having tried this type 2 in printing the *Quatre Derrenieres Choses*, and being satisfied with its appearance, Caxton had packed it up and brought it with him to England.

Settled at Westminster, he lost no time in getting to work. One of his successors,

Robert Copland, stated that his "worshipful master, Caxton," began by printing "small storyes and pamflets and so to other." At Copland's death in 1548, it was said that he was the oldest printer in England, so that he might very well have worked in Caxton's office as a boy; at any rate he was closely associated with Caxton's successor, Wynkyn de Worde, not only printing books but doing a great deal of literary work for him. Copland therefore had every opportunity of gaining knowledge of Caxton's methods and work, and his statement has been confirmed by a striking discovery.

Amongst the books in the library of the University of Cambridge, bequeathed to it by Bishop Moore, was one, which until it was examined by that unrivalled bibliographer, Henry Bradshaw of Cambridge, had been thought to consist of one work only. It was found to contain eight "small storyes or pamflets," averaging about twenty quarto leaves each, all of them printed by Caxton with type No. 2, but without any date. The pieces in this volume were *Anelide and Arcite* and *The Temple of Brass*, both from the pen of Geoffrey Chaucer; *Stans Puer ad Mensam, The Chorle and the Bird, The Horse, the Shepe and the Ghoos* and *The Temple of Glas*, all by John Lydgate; *Parvus and Magnus Catho*, already referred to as the work of the Canon of St. Stephens; and finally the *Boke of Courtesy*, by an unknown author, who confessed himself a disciple of Lydgate. This volume was afterwards broken up and the eight pieces are now separately bound.

While admitting that these small publications are all printed " in the early state of type 2," Wm. Blades assigned most of them to the year 1479; but from his own admission, coupled with Copland's statement, there is little doubt that they were the first-fruits of Caxton's press, and were probably printed some in 1476 and some in 1477.

What better literature could Caxton have

found in any language to put into circulation? The *Stans Puer ad Mensam,* the *Cato* and the *Boke of Courtesy* were written for the instruction of youth, and taught the values of virtue, knowledge, cleanliness and sobriety: the remainder were pleasant poems and romances written for the delight of older readers, by two of the most popular of English authors. Yet we are asked to believe that Caxton did nothing to form the taste of his English readers, that he was the slave of his so-called "patrons," and was actuated by no higher motives than his own personal gain.[1] But his critics carefully refrain from telling us what they think he could or ought to have printed. True, one of them suggested that he might have printed the Bible in English, being obviously unaware that Caxton was a staunch Catholic and that the Church of Rome had repeatedly forbidden the translation of the Scriptures into English. With the exception of the

[1] *The Library,* September, 1922. "The First English Printers and their Patrons," by Professor H. B. Lathrop.

Cato, all these pieces were chosen by Caxton himself, and from the fact that second editions of several of them were called for immediately, we may infer that he had accurately gauged the requirements of the reading public. His object in beginning with these little poems and educational works was clearly to pay his running expenses while more important and larger books were being prepared, and it in no way minimizes the value of Caxton's work for England that he ran, or endeavoured to run, his press on business lines. The greater part of his life had been spent in trade, he had acquired business habits, which he would naturally apply to his new undertaking; but its monetary success, if not a matter of indifference to him, was, we believe, entirely overshadowed by his desire to print for the benefit of his countrymen, not only the best literature which that country produced, but the best literature, moral, historical or romantic, that he could come by. As an example of this, one of the very earliest books that came from his press was a book of Hours, the first prayer-book printed in this country, and the first book printed on vellum. Its format was small, only twelve lines being printed to a full page, it is made up in quires of eight leaves, and there are eight quires remaining. It shows all the peculiarities of Caxton's early work, and is without signatures, numbers to pages, or head-lines.[1]

From the fact that it contained prayers to the Three Kings of Cologne and to St. Barbara, not usually found in the *Horæ* of that period, it is believed to have been printed for the German merchants of the Hanseatic League in London, whose patron saint was St. Barbara, and who used the prayer to the three kings as being specially applicable to merchants and travellers.

While superintending the printing of these and other small things, Caxton had been busy translating another Troy book into

[1] E. G. Duff. *Horæ beate virginio Marie secundum usum Sarum.* The unique copy printed at Westminster by William Caxton *circa* 1477. 1908, 8vo.

English, *The History of Jason*, a sequel to the *Recuyell of the Historyes of Troye*, which he had printed in Bruges. It is just possible that he had begun the translation of *Jason* while he was still abroad, and that he undertook it as a compliment to Margaret, Duchess of Burgundy, who had encouraged him to persevere with the translation of the earlier work; but he also felt that, dealing as it did with chivalry and the foundation of the Order of the Golden Fleece, it would please English readers, who delighted in feats of arms, and in addition to this, as he pointed out in his Prologue, there was much novelty in the histories and much that was good for a young man to know. With the permission of the King and Queen he dedicated the book to the Prince of Wales, then about four years of age, "to thentente that he may begynne to lerne rede English."

The *Book of Jason* was a folio of 150 leaves, printed in type 2, without date, pagination, head-lines, signatures or colophon, and Mr. Duff gave it as his opinion that it was the first large book which Caxton issued in England.

The first of his publications in which the date of printing was given was the *Dictes or Sayengis of the Philosophres*, the printing of which was finished on the 18th November, 1477. This was a translation of a French work entitled *Les Dits Moraux des Philosophes,* made by Earl Rivers, who had known Caxton for some years, and knowing his literary tastes, asked him to "oversee" his translation before printing it, a task which Caxton very readily undertook. The nature of the work was clearly set out by the Earl in his Preface. It contained, he said, "great comfort to every well disposed soul." "It lauds virtue and science; it blames vice and ignorance." Caxton found it a book after his own heart, but in reading it he found that the Earl had omitted certain sayings of Socrates "towchying women," and supposes that "the wynde had blowe over the leefe" while the translator was at work, and caused its omission. Apparently the Earl took no offence at the insertion by Caxton of Socrates' opinion of women, which was not a high one. Whether the printer shared those views or whether, as some think, he was having a sly dig at the Earl, is an open question. Caxton certainly admired educated women, and when a few months later Earl Rivers sent him the manuscript of a translation which he had made of *Les Prouerbes Moraulx,* composed by Cristyne de Pise, Caxton printed the book under the title, *The Moral Proverbs of Cristyne,* on the 22nd February, 1477/8. The authoress was one of the most gifted women of her time. She was married at the early age of fifteen, and within a few years was left a widow with three children and nothing to support them. As her *Proverbs* and other writings showed, she was a woman of great piety and indomitable will.

Here again Caxton showed his judgment. The high character of the work ensured its popularity, not only amongst the clergy, whom as we have seen were by far the largest class of book-buyers, but with all right thinking and God-fearing men and women.

But the most important as well as the largest book which Caxton printed with type No. 2, that is, during the first two years of his establishment at Westminster, was *The Canterbury Tales* of Geoffrey Chaucer. The work must have taxed the capabilities of his press and workmen heavily, as it consisted of no less than 374 leaves and made a stout folio. Like all his early work it was without adornment of any kind, neither title page, ornament, initial letters or illustrations: but it was the first time Chaucer's great work had appeared in print. Unadorned as it was, this was surely a piece of work of which Caxton might be proud, and of which Englishmen too may also be proud. There is no hint of any "patrons'" influence over the printer to induce him to produce this book: his love of his country, coupled with his love of good literature, were incentives enough. His zeal indeed led him to be somewhat too hasty in the choice of the manuscript, and much to his grief and annoyance, he afterwards found out that the text he had printed was a corrupt one.

This brings us naturally to the question: How many copies went to an edition in Caxton's time? He gives us no help. In referring to this first edition of *The Canterbury Tales*, he says, "I dyde do enprynte a certayn nombre of them, whyche anon were sold to many and dyverse gentylmen." The only evidence we have upon which to base any kind of estimate is that of Richard Pynson, who began as a printer in the parish of St. Clement Danes about 1490, and who brought an action against a certain John Russhe, Esquire, to recover a debt incurred by him, for the printing at his desire of various books, some of them as early as 1492. From this it appeared that an agreement was entered into between them by which Pynson printed six hundred copies of the *Dives and Pauper*, and the same number of Boccaccio's *Falle of Princes*, of which number Russhe agreed to take half. Both these books were smaller than *The Canterbury Tales,* and doubtless the size had something to do with determining the number of copies to be printed, as the working expenses, wages, paper, wear and tear of type, etc., would be greater in the case of a work of three hundred leaves than in a work of only thirty, and the edition would have to be large enough to cover these. On the other hand, Pynson had disposed of half his six hundred copies before he started to print, and in the absence of any such guarantee, probably Caxton's first edition of *The Canterbury Tales* was about three hundred copies.

CHAPTER VI

Making the road—Caxton's friends not "patrons"—His judgment in the choice of books—Arrival of other printers in England—Effects of their rivalry—Books issued by Caxton between 1479 and 1482.

THE introduction of printing into England was welcomed as a burst of sunshine after a cold and dreary winter. It brought light and warmth and freedom to a people who had sat long in darkness. It created a thirst for knowledge and produced the long line of distinguished writers that mark the literary history of England.

Anthony Wydeville and his friends were not Caxton's "patrons"; they were contributors to a great national work, the laying of the road to freedom of thought, freedom of speech and liberty such as no other nation can boast.

It may be asked: Would Caxton have dared to refuse a manuscript offered him by

Earl Rivers? He certainly would have done so if the occasion had arisen; but such a position cannot be conceived. Neither Earl Rivers nor any one of Caxton's many admirers would have thought of offering him an ill-written or immoral book to print. They knew their man and he knew them.

We may brush aside Caxton's phrases about their "great rewards" to him and all the rest of it. Like the ruff and the farthingale, such language was the fashion of the time. Does any sane man or woman believe that "a buck in winter and a doe in summer," or whichever it was, paid Caxton's wages bill for a week? A sheep could be bought for three shillings in those days, and a buck probably cost not more than ten shillings, and even if these prices be multiplied twenty times in order to equal the value of money at the present day, it amounted to very little. His customers, peer and commoner alike, paid him for his work as a printer; but he was under no sort of obligation to them, and Caxton was just the man to print a good book, even if he lost by it, rather than his countrymen should want it. His judgment in the choice of books was sound. Before the end of 1478 twenty-one books can be traced to his press. One work believed to have been printed during that time—Ovid's *Metamorphosis*—has perished entirely, and no doubt many of his "short storyes and pamflets" have shared the same fate. Looking down the list of those that have come down to us whole or in part, we find philosophical works, books for the young, service books, devotional works, poems and romances, and of these seven went into a second edition, and one, the *Parvus et Magnus Catho,* into a third.

But Caxton was not allowed to remain long the sole printer in England. Perhaps attracted by rumours of his success, or, possibly invited over by some in authority at the University, an unknown printer made his appearance in Oxford in 1478. But he was too far away to trouble Caxton. Then, about 1479, we hear of that mysterious "schoolmaster printer of St. Albans," to whom we have already alluded, and about whom it is sincerely to be hoped that we shall one day know more. Whoever he was, his relations with Caxton were rather friendly than otherwise, and he does not appear to have been a very formidable rival. Much more serious was the arrival in 1480 of a foreign printer named John Lettou, a native of Lithuania, who set up in the City of London, and in that year issued a book in folio entitled *Antonius Andreæ, Questiones super XII, libros metaphysicæ*, at the desire of a certain William Wilcock, whose identity has never been established and who is never heard of again.

It at once became evident that the new printer had learnt his art under a much better master than Caxton had. The type in which that book was printed was a neat gothic, and each page was printed in double columns. The lines were spaced out and signatures were used.

Early in the year Caxton had printed an

Indulgence, by Pope Sixtus IV, to all who would contribute to the defence of Rhodes. This he printed in his large type, but Lettou immediately issued two other editions of the same indulgence, and the comparison was in Lettou's favour.

The competition of these various rivals woke Caxton up to the necessity of showing more interest in the mechanical side of his art. Accordingly, between the years 1478 and 1481, he effected certain changes for the better. The type that he had been using ever since his settlement at Westminster was getting worn, so he trimmed it and recast some of the letters.[1]

In 1479 he began to use an entirely different fount of type, to which the name of Black Letter has been applied. It was a particularly bold and handsome letter, modelled on those cast by the early German printers, Fust and Schoeffer. It was eminently suited to the printing of service books for the Church and other works in

[1] This variation of type 2 was known as type 2*.

Latin, for which purpose Caxton used it, no English book in this type being known, neither is there any complete copy of any book printed with it. Consequently the dates during which it was in use are more or less a matter of conjecture.

The most important work printed with this type, from the point of view of what remains of it, is a *Psalterium* in quarto. In addition to the Psalms it included the Canticles, Te Deum, Athanasian Creed and Litany, and as its use was general throughout England, Caxton's edition was possibly a large one. The *Sarum Ordinale* or *Pica*, sometimes called the *Directorium Sacerdotum*, was also printed with this type, but only a few fragments of it are known. Its purpose was to show the officiating priest what lessons or prayers were to be read on Saints' days, such a guide being necessary owing to the ever changing variations in the Feast of Easter. It was in connection with this that Caxton printed with the same type the well-known advertisement :

"If it plese ony man spiritual or temporal to bye ony pyes of two and three comemoracions of salisburie use, enpryntid after the forme of this present lettre, whiche ben wel and truly correct, late hym come to westmonester in to the almonetrye at the reed pale and he shal have them good chepe."

This was not only the first broadside printed in this country, but also the first book advertisement. It also for the first time makes mention of the "Red Pale" as the sign of Caxton's printing house. It also had this further peculiarity. At the foot of the advertisement, printed in Latin, was an appeal to the public not to tear it down, an act which was more likely to be committed by a person ignorant of Latin.

The only other work printed entirely in this Black Letter type was a book of Hours, of which also only a few fragments have been found.

In printing these service books Caxton did useful work. They were in constant demand, and hundreds of copies could be turned out by the printing-press in less time than it would have taken a scrivener to write one. Besides this they gave employment to his workmen, and as a practical business man he could not neglect such an obvious source of income; but his ambition was not to put money in his pocket, but to use his press mainly for broadening the foundations of knowledge by printing books of a more general character.

For this reason perhaps, Caxton gave up the use of this Black Letter type, except for head-lines in conjunction with other types. In this way it helps to fix the date of printing of the Boëthius' *De Consolatione Philosophie*, for several reasons one of the most notable books that ever came from Caxton's press. In the first place the translation was the work of Chaucer, whom Caxton delighted to honour, and whose work he took pride in circulating in print amongst his countrymen. Again, the *De Consolatione* was famed throughout Europe. There were copies of it in every library, and it had been translated into many languages. Caxton foresaw equal popularity for it in England, and he must have printed an unusually large edition, as at the present time no less than twenty-six copies of it are still in existence, besides several fragments and imperfect copies. Further, Caxton's biographer, William Blades, in the summer of 1858, discovered an uncut copy of this book in its original binding in a cupboard in the library of the Grammar School of the Abbey of St. Albans. The boards with which the book was bound were found to consist of waste sheets from Caxton's office, and amongst these were the fragments of the *Sarum Ordinale* and the *Horæ* just mentioned, the existence of which had never previously been heard of.

In order to meet Lettou's competition, Caxton, in 1480, began to use signatures and to space out his lines to an even length. He also, probably for the same reason, brought into use his type 4, which was modelled on type 2, but was smaller and altogether neater in appearance.

Looking round for some work with which to test this new fount, Caxton turned out the long-forgotten vocabulary in French and English which he had amused himself by making while he was on the Continent, and to which reference has been made in Chapter II. That he did not rate the work very highly is shown by the fact that he did not trouble to revise the text, did not put his name to it, and ended it up abruptly with the words :

> Here endeth this doctrine,
> At westmestre, by London,
> In fourmes enprinted.

But it was a useful little work, and after Caxton's death Wynkyn de Worde reprinted it.

Meanwhile, at the request of divers gentlemen, he put to press and finished on the 10th June, 1480, an historical work which he called *The Chronicles of England*. The basis of the work was the *Chronicle of Brute,* and Caxton added a continuation that brought it down to the battle of Towton. It came to be known as *Caxton's Chronicle*. As a sequel to this he published a few months later, also in folio, the *Description of*

Britain, a chapter out of Ralph Higden's *Polychronicon*.

During the year 1481 the road was carried forward still further by the addition to the English language of several interesting and valuable works. Although no longer a mercer by trade, Caxton kept in touch with many of his old associates, and during a visit to one of these, Hugh Brice, who was just then a notable man in the City of London, Brice told his friend that he was anxious to make some sort of gift to Lord Hastings, in return for many favours received from that nobleman, and thought that the present should take the form of a book. He then brought out a French translation of a Latin work called *Speculum vel Imago Mundi*, and asked Caxton if he would undertake to turn it into English and print it, in which case Brice undertook to pay the costs of printing. In this instance the choice was not Caxton's, nor was he called upon to exercise any judgment in the matter, Hugh Brice being as well-read a man as Caxton himself, and there was no question as to the suitability of the work for English readers. The work was an epitome of universal knowledge, so far as human knowledge had up to that time progressed, and dealt not only with the creation of the world, but also how the seven sciences were founded and what they were. It dealt with the various divisions of the world, and contained descriptions of Europe, Asia and Africa, their inhabitants and the birds and animals common to each. As the book was intended as a present to a nobleman, stress was laid by the translator on the appeal it made to the hearts of nobles, but Caxton would have been the first to deny that in accepting Hugh Brice's invitation to translate it he intended it only for one class of readers. Indeed, he makes this clear in his Prologue, when he says, "Thenne who so wylle comprise and vnderstande the substance of this present volume," etc., and further on, "Thenne let vs praye" to God Almighty for wisdom to understand the book, the word "us" being clearly applied to all those who were sufficiently educated to be able to read it. To men and women who could not read the book would only appeal by teaching orally, and Caxton evidently was thinking of this, when in his prayer he asked for divine grace, not only to remember what he read, but that by remembering he might be able to teach it to others. Caxton began the translation on the 2nd January, 1480/1, and finished it on the 8th March following, and printed it under "the shadow of the noble protection" of King Edward IV.

The Mirrour of the World was a folio of 100 leaves, printed with the earlier form of type, and the lines are fully spaced out. It was the first of Caxton's books that was illustrated, two sets of wood-cuts being used in it, one illustrating a master and scholars, and the other consisting of diagrams that were so poorly executed that the printer could not understand them, and placed them in wrong positions.

Caxton followed up *The Mirrour of the*

World with Cicero's famous treatise *De Senectute*. When translating the *Recuyell of the Histories of Troy*, he had talked about age creeping on him and enfeebling his body, although as nearly as we can tell he was then in the prime of life, and if his complaint was anything more than assumed, we can only suppose that he was not a strong man. At any rate here we find him returning to the subject of old age and giving the public Cicero's book, a work that still ranks amongst the world's famous classics. It had been translated into English some years before at the instance of Sir John Falstofe, to whom Caxton pays his due meed of praise. The translator has never been discovered, and copies of the manuscript were evidently very scarce, as Caxton tells us that it was only after great labour and cost that he had been able to get a copy; but on account of its high literary value, as well as the wisdom contained in its pages, he had printed it, that noble, virtuous and well-disposed men who were getting on in years might have it to console themselves with. It was not a book for youths or frivolous minded people, nor for those who had never heard of the greatness of Rome.

It was directed to those who had passed their green youth, and showed them how to bear the trials of old age with patience. How can it be said that Caxton did nothing to form public taste when he put into print such a notable book as this?

It is true there were a few manuscripts of this English translation in existence; but, evidently, very few and hard to come by. To all intents and purposes it was unknown to the majority of English readers. As a book likely to provide food for thought and to be a great moral and intellectual force is the best justification of Caxton's choice of it.

To the *De Senectute* Caxton added the same writer's *De Amitia* or *Treatise on Friendship*, on the ground that there cannot be a better thing annexed to old age than true friendship.

The translation of the *De Amitia* into English had been made by John Tiptoft, Earl of Worcester, a great soldier, a great statesman, and a great collector of books. The Earl was an adherent of the House of York, and was captured and executed during the brief return to power of Henry VI in 1470. Caxton laments his death in a touching passage in his final Epilogue.

To round off the whole he added to the two preceding works the *Declamation of Noblesse,* made by Scipio and Flaminius before the Roman Senate. Presumably Caxton translated this himself, and John Leland, the antiquary, who was a good Latinist, described it as terse, neat and significant, and doubted whether the author of them wrote or Caxton translated with greater grace. This passage may be commended to the notice of those who doubt the printer's ability to translate Latin.

The three treatises made a folio volume of 117 leaves or 234 pages. It was dedicated to the King, and was printed towards the latter end of 1481. Altogether it was a book of which Caxton as printer and editor might well be proud.

Another of the issues of 1481 was an even more remarkable book. Hitherto the books that had come from the press at Westminster, good as they were, dealt for the most part with subjects of popular interest. But for some time past Caxton had been at work on a translation of the great German satire *Reineke Fuchs*. None of Caxton's critics have been able to show any outside influence exercised upon the printer to induce him to translate and print this book. It was entirely his own choice, and is another instance of his far-seeing judgment in the matter of good literature. The work had long been a classic on the continent of Europe, and like the *De Consolatione Philosophie* of Boëthius had been translated into many languages. Caxton used a Dutch manuscript, possibly one purchased while he was in Bruges. In some respects it was a daring venture on his part. As the late

Professor J. A. Froude pointed out in an essay on *Reynard the Fox*, the poem was not merely a clever and witty satire on the world and on the men whom the world delights to honour. There was something deeper in it than that. Superficially, its morality was doubtful, and Caxton was careful to echo the warning of the author, that his readers were not to follow Reynard's methods, but to eschew evil and do good; but it was a book to be read and read again, and if Caxton had done no more than translate and print this book, it would have been of more value than a barrow full of classics. He took the risk and again his judgment was justified, as the book went into a second edition before his death.

From satire Caxton passed to chivalry, and followed up *Reynard the Fox* with *The History of Godfrey of Boloyne,* or *The Conquest of Jerusalem.* He appears to have been moved to undertake this translation by the events which were then taking place in Europe, notably the siege of Rhodes by the

Turks, and his aim was to arouse the martial spirit of the kings and people of Christendom to combine together for the overthrow of the Turks, and to emulate the valorous deeds of King Arthur of Britain, Charlemagne of France, and Godfrey of Boloyne. Once again a higher purpose is revealed in Caxton's work than mere money-getting. In making this translation he used a French manuscript, of which there were many in his time. There is one in the Bibliothèque Nationale in Paris which belonged to Louis de Bruges, in whose library Caxton may have seen it. There is another now in the British Museum, and the text of both of these agrees with his translation.

From chivalry to history is a natural transition, and the next important publication that came from the "Red Pale" was Ralph Higden's *Polychronicon*. In many respects this was the most ambitious of all Caxton's undertakings up till that time. Not only did he revise the text throughout, but he added a continuation from the year 1357 down to the accession of King Edward IV in 1460.

As its title implies, it was a compilation from many chronicles and works on natural history, in Latin, by Ralph Higden, a monk of St. Werburg in Chester. Some modern writers hold that it was a "crib" from an earlier work by another monk of the same monastery; but Humphrey Wanley, librarian to the Earl of Oxford in the eighteenth century and one of the cleverest men of his day, was not of that opinion. Higden it was who called the work *Polychronicon.* It was next taken in hand by Trevisa, chaplain to Lord Barkeley, and by him translated in 1387 out of Latin into English prose. It was Trevisa's version that Caxton upon his own initiative, but under the "noble protection" of the King, took in hand, and in order to bring it up-to-date, compiled a continuation to the beginning of that king's reign. The work is preceded by a "Proheme" written by Caxton, which fills four folio pages and extols the value of histories and the merit due to those who compile them. History, he tells us, is the mother of all philosophy, and because it is so precious and profitable he has undertaken to write two books, of which this is one. What happened to the other, which ought to have preceded it, will be told in its place. The "Proheme" finishes:

"And nowe at thys tyme simply emprinted and set in forme,[1] by me William Caxton and a lytle embellished from the old making, and also have added such stories as I could find from the end that the said Ranulph finished his book, which was the year of our lord 1357 unto the year of the same 1460, which be a hundred and three year, which work I have finished vnder the noble protection of my most dread, natural and sovereign lord and most Christian King, King Edward the Fourth, humbly beseeching his most noble grace to pardon me if any

[1] A phrase possibly borrowed from the printing house, a page being set in a "forme" before being printed.

thing be said therein of ignorance, or otherwise than it ought to be. And also requiring all other to amend whereas there is default, wherein he or they may deserve thank and merit, and I shall pray for them that so do, for I knowledge my ignorance and also simplenes. And if there be thing that may please or profit any man, I am glad that I have achieved it. Of which accomplishing, I thank Almighty God. To whom be given honour, laud and glory, in secula seculorum. Amen."

This was written by the man whom we are now asked to believe did nothing to guide public taste in books, and was moved by nothing higher than his commercial interests!

On the last leaf of the seventh book he tells us a little more about its preparation. As few people then wrote in their "registers," meaning possibly the bishops and abbots, there was, he foresaw, a danger that many interesting events which had taken place since Trevisa's days might be forgotten. So he set to work and compiled this addition. The only books of reference he could find were two in Latin, the *Fasciculus Temporum* and *Aureus de Universo*, but they were of little use to him, and as the bulk of this last book deals with English matters, he must have relied on information supplied by those whose fathers and grandfathers had been living at the time or upon his own knowledge.

The extract already given may serve as an example of Caxton's style as a writer; but as this is his first appearance as an historian, the following description of the marriage of Margaret of Anjou to King Henry VI in 1444 is worth reprinting:[1]

"In this year king harry maried at Southweke quene Margaret, And she came to London the eighteenth day of May.

"And by the way all the lords of England

[1] In this and the preceding passage the old spelling has been modernized for the greater comfort of the reader.

received her worshipfully in divers places, and in especial the Duke of Gloucester. And on Blackheath the mayor, aldermen and all the crafts in blue gowns embroidered with the device of his craft that they might be be-known, met with her with red hoods, and brought her to London, where were divers pageants and countenances of divers histories shewed in divers places of the city, royally and costly. And the thirtyest (30th) day of May the said queen was crowned at Westminster. And there was jousts three days during within the sanctuary to fore (=before) the Abbey."

Caxton finished the compilation and editing of the *Polychronicon* on the 2nd July, 1482, and the work was printed soon after. The edition must have been a large one, as no less than eighty-eight more or less perfect copies and ten fragments are recorded in De Ricci's *Census of Caxton*, as existing at the present day. Another interesting point about this book is that the marginal notes are put in in red ink. This writing is contemporary; but the handwriting has not been identified.

About this time Caxton issued a second edition of one of his earlier books, *The Game and Playe of the Chess*. The first edition had been printed at Bruges without date, either in 1474 or 1475. This was another of Caxton's self-imposed tasks, for the translation had been made by him from the French. Under the guise of a game of chess, the book consisted of a number of short stories told by ancient doctors, philosophers and poets, with a moral tendency. To this second edition he added illustrations, twenty-four in number, very poorly drawn and cut for the most part, yet in their way helping to visualize the stories to which they are prefixed. These wood-cuts were executed in England, and when we look at them it is not surprising that Caxton called in the aid of the wood-cutters so seldom.

CHAPTER VII

Caxton's work as "roadmaker" continued—Success of his press—Takes additional premises—Notable books issued between 1483 and 1487—*De Confessio Amantis*—*Golden Legend*—English poems—*Æsop*—Caxton's complaint of the decay of chivalry—His "conversations" with his customers—Westminster Hall a haunt of literary men—*Morte d'Arthur*—Death of his friend William Pratt — Caxton's device.

DURING the seven years that had elapsed since Caxton settled at Westminster his business as a printer had steadily increased. His competitors, such as they were, either dropped out after a year or two's work, or like the London printer, Lettou, found that the printing of classical works did not pay and devoted themselves to a special class of work, the printing of law books, which Caxton was only too pleased to leave to them. In the issue of general literature, catering for the tastes of a variety of readers, he had the field to himself.

It is not surprising, then, that by the year

1483 he found the "Red Pale" too small for his requirements, and rented from the Abbot a second "tenement," the position of which is not disclosed, at a rental of 3s. 4d. per year, and also secured a loft over the gateway of the Almonry. There are no records telling us how many presses he had or how many hands he employed at that time, but he was not only printing books but binding them, and it is possible that he transferred his "bindery" to the new premises, while consigning to the loft his stock of paper and unsold books, thus leaving the "Red Pale" free for the printers and compositors. Not only so, but about this time he began to issue profusely illustrated books, and if, as seems likely, he employed his own woodcutters, room had to be found for them also.

During the five years now to be considered, Caxton's efforts, both as printer and translator, reached their maximum. Some of the largest books he had yet printed were produced during this time, while his labours as translator and editor were unceasing.

In 1483 he printed three books, averaging one hundred and fifty folios, i.e., three hundred pages each, besides smaller books such as the *Sex Epistolæ*, and this average he kept up, aiming all the while at higher things.

His first dated issue in 1483 was a book for the clergy, the *Festial* or *Liber Festivalis*. This was not a service book, it was rather in the nature of a preacher's assistant, containing stories from the *Golden Legend* and a similar work called the *Gesta Romanorum*, which could be used as the foundation for sermons.

The *Festial* was compiled by John Mirkus, a canon of the monastery of Lilleshul in Shropshire, and its contents included a list of those whose souls might and ought to be prayed for, notably, "those who had been kings of this realm of England," and all persons who had given book, bell, or candle to the Church. As a sequel to the *Festial*, Caxton also printed four sermons or homilies for use in connection with it.

These two books may have been a speculation on the printer's part, on the other hand the Abbot of Westminster or some of the higher clergy may have suggested to him that such a publication would be of great use and supply a long-felt want.

The *Festial* was dated the last day of June, and on September 2nd Caxton gave his countrymen "a bok for Englandes sake," John Gower's *Confessio Amantis* or *Lovers' Confession*. The poet's object was to bring pleasure and profit to his readers, so he combined the parts of troubadour and historian, and mixed with his love songs stories reciting the virtues and vices of rulers. There is little doubt that the demand for copies of Gower's poem was greater than the copyists could meet, and Caxton did a public service by printing it. His critics argue that in printing such works as the *Canterbury Tales* and the *Confessio Amantis* he was simply following public taste, not leading it. Let us examine this argument a little more closely.

When preparing for the Early English Text Society *The English Works of John Gower*, in 1900, Mr. G. C. Macauley discovered and described forty-five English manuscripts of the *Confessio Amantis* written in the fifteenth century. Let us say that one hundred copies of the poem were in circulation in Caxton's day. It has already been shown that the number of educated persons able to read was much larger than is generally supposed. But how many of them had ever heard of Gower and his work? To say that the *Confessio Amantis* was "widely known" when only one hundred persons out of several thousands possessed copies is to exaggerate. You cannot be said to have a taste for a thing that you have never seen or heard of. As a matter of fact, the early printers were entirely in the dark as to the number of readers for whom they ought to cater. They knew that a certain number of the nobility and a certain number of the clergy were book collectors; but they had no idea how many people outside that privileged circle were eager to have books. So they limited their issues to six hundred copies, and this was probably the number that Caxton printed of the *Confessio Amantis*. By so doing he brought the work to the knowledge of five hundred additional people who up to that time were either totally ignorant of its existence or had been unable to secure a manuscript copy. Those five hundred probably meant the creation of five or six hundred more appetites, and by multiplying the number of existing copies from one hundred to seven hundred he laid the road to greater demand, so that when, in 1553, his successor, Thomas Berthelet, once more issued the book, the edition was immediately snapped up and another had to be put to press the following year. To one of these printed editions of the *Confessio Amantis*, Shakespeare went for the plot of *Pericles*, one of the most human and delightful of his plays—a striking instance of where the road led that Caxton laid down.

Another of the issues of the year 1483

was the *Golden Legend*, the largest book that Caxton had so far printed, a folio of 447 printed leaves or 894 pages, printed in double columns of 55 lines. The types used were the small Gothic, distinguished as type 4*, with the Black Letter type for head-lines and headings to chapters. The work was also illustrated with a frontispiece and eighteen large and fifty-two small wood-cuts.

The *Golden Legend* was the other historical work which Caxton had in hand at the time of the publication of *Polychronicon*. Its compilation had proved a far heavier task than he had anticipated, and he foresaw that a heavy outlay would be necessary to see it through the press. At this point the history of the *Recuyell* repeats itself. Despairing of ever getting it finished, he had made up his mind to abandon the task—it was a self-imposed one and not a commission—when one day William Fitzallan, the Earl of Arundel, walked into the "Red Pale," and in the course of conversation asked Caxton how he was getting on with the *Golden Legend*.

In reply Caxton told him that he found the task beyond his powers, and proposed to drop it. The Earl asked to see what he had done, and in order to encourage him to carry the work through, promised to take a certain number of copies when it was printed, and as a compliment added that he would instruct his steward to send the printer a buck in summer and a doe in winter. No doubt Caxton highly appreciated this addition to his larder, and he paid the Earl the usual exaggerated lip-service in the Prologue, but its intrinsic value was *nil.* Nor does Caxton tell us how many copies the Earl offered to take. None the less it was a sporting offer, and had the effect which it was intended to have; it encouraged Caxton to see the thing through, and no doubt he printed a larger edition than usual on the strength of the Earl's promise, as it is one of the commonest of all Caxton's books. The *Golden Legend* was not undertaken either at the " command " or " request " of the Earl of Arundel. Its compilation and publication had been decided on by the printer, so far as we know, without consultation with anyone, and in this case the Earl was a helper rather than a "patron."

A very clever study of the *Golden Legend* was undertaken by Dr. Pierce Butler of the John Hopkin's University, Baltimore, U.S.A., in 1899, and in the course of it he points out that to the legends of the Saints Caxton added a large number of Bible stories. To quote his own words: "This portion of Caxton's *Golden Legend* is little more than a disguised version of the Bible. He dared not publish the Bible as such, for that would smell of Wycliff and rank Lollardy, and Caxton had no ambition to stir up the powers that were in Church or State; but he evaded the vigilance of the laws by inserting Bible stories in his *Golden Legend*." Dr. Butler also puts forward the suggestion that the *Golden Legend* became "one of the principal instruments in preparing the way for the Reformation." If this theory can be accepted, it gives additional value to

Caxton's work. To Dr. Butler also belongs the credit of being the first to call attention to the little glimpses of Caxton while on the Continent, which are introduced into the *Golden Legend*, and which have already been mentioned in Chapter II.

Caxton went to three sources for his work, a Latin manuscript of Jacobus de Voragine, an English manuscript, and apparently a printed copy of the translation by Jehan de Vignay, called *La Légende Dorée*.[1] Many of the stories or legends in the Latin and French versions were not in the English, and it is evident that Caxton drew on other sources for some of his incidents.

In estimating the value of this great work upon which Caxton spent so much thought, time, patience and research, it must be remembered that England was then a Roman Catholic country, and that it was also a superstitious age. From the lowest to the

[1] *Legenda Aurea—Légende Dorée—Golden Legend.* A study of Caxton's *Golden Legend*, with special reference to its relations to the earlier English prose translation, by Pierce Butler, Fellow in English at the John Hopkin's University, Baltimore, 1899, pp. 81, 82.

highest, all classes believed in relics and miracles, and consequently lives of the Saints were considered the most wholesome reading. Tales of wonder, of hardship, of miraculous escapes and cruel deaths served to while away many a long dark winter's evening, apart altogether from their religious teaching, and they probably sowed the seeds which bore fruit in their readers or hearers, making pilgrimages to famous shrines.

To this time also belongs one of the few political pamphlets printed by Caxton, the *Sex Quam Elegantissimæ Epistolæ*, a series of letters that passed between Pope Sixtus IV and the Venetian Republic. The printing was probably commissioned and paid for by the Venetian ambassador.

In 1483, or 1484, he went back to the English poets, and printed Lydgate's *Life of Our Lady*, and Chaucer's *House of Fame* and *Troilus and Cressida,* as well as a second edition of the *Canterbury Tales.* Lydgate's devotional poem had been composed at the desire of King Henry V. At the end Caxton added a stanza in verse, praying his readers to pardon any faults they found in the printed copy, a form of "envoy" which William Blades pointed out was common to writers of that age, and did not imply any serious omissions in the text.

To the *House of Fame* he added an Epilogue extolling Chaucer for the wisdom and subtle understanding contained in the poem, and expressing his opinion that Chaucer excelled all other English writers. He used no unmeaning words, and his "matter" was full of "hye and quycke sentence," so much so that other writers had borrowed from him freely.

In choosing this poem as one of his publications, Caxton showed that his aim was to educate as well as to amuse his readers. The same purpose led him to publish the second edition of the *Canterbury Tales*. It had been pointed out to him by a purchaser of the first edition that the copy he had used was a poor one, and his informant at the same time said that his father had a much better manuscript, which he would try and let the printer see. Caxton replied that in that case he would undertake to reprint the work. This he did, and in order to increase the attractiveness of the book he illustrated it with cuts of the various pilgrims. These illustrations were probably cut in Caxton's office, and while they show some improvement on those found in earlier books, they are very inferior to the work of the Continental wood-cutters.

In addition to all this, and not content with the task of translating the *Polychronicon* and the *Golden Legend*, Caxton had been at work on another book that he thought English people would appreciate, and which would afford them both delight and instruction, and early in 1484 issued the *Fables of Æsop*, illustrated with a frontispiece and any amount of cuts, which in themselves, badly cut as they are, add to the charm of this wonderful old book. In this *Æsop* also appeared for the first time in any of Caxton's books a wood-cut initial. Mr. E. Gordon

Duff described this as one of the finest and rarest of all Caxton's publications.

In the Prologue to the second edition of Cato's *Distiches*, which he printed towards the latter end of 1483, Caxton lamented the degeneracy of the young men of London. We still hear the same complaints to-day, and we know there is nothing in them. Caxton had grown old and failed to make allowance for the change in manners and customs since he was a young man. The youth of 1483 were quite the equals of the youth of 1438, just as the young men of 1924 are, and have proved themselves, not only equal but superior to the youths of 1824.

There was much more truth in Caxton's lament for the decay of chivalry, although in this case again he forgot that chivalry had not altered but custom and circumstances had, and that the old feudal system that compelled every tenant of a lord to supply horse and man when called upon, and every lord to supply the king with a company of armed men, was passing away never to return. We can, nevertheless, sympathize with him. He loved to see jousts and tournaments, and believed quite rightly that chivalry was a high ideal of which knightly qualities were one of the expressions, and he felt sorry to see them going out of use. So about this time he translated and printed two books in the hope of reviving them. The first was a quarto of only fifty-two leaves entitled *The Book of the Order of Chivalry or Knighthode*, the other was Sir Thomas Malory's *Morte d'Arthur*, one of the most famous books that issued from Caxton's printing house.

But it was not his own inclination alone that led him to undertake this work. It was partly the result of conversations that had taken place with several persons who had strongly urged the printer to issue more books of that character, and an interesting question arises, where did those conversations take place?

There is no doubt that by this time

Caxton's printing office had become the meeting place of the *literati*. Lords and ladies from the Court, the clergy of London, merchants from the city, and book lovers of every class found their way there, to buy books and talk over bookish matters with the old printer. But there was another place in Westminster where men did congregate, and where Caxton no doubt often met men and women interested in books, and that was the great Hall where the King's courts of law were held, and which during term time was thronged with large numbers of people from all parts of the country, in fact it was one of the busiest spots in the neighbourhood of London. Barristers and lawyers in wigs and gowns, lawyers' clerks carrying bundles of books and documents, bustled in and out all day long, while many of those who strolled up and down the Hall were mere idlers. Here and there about the Hall were stalls, chiefly those of stationers who sold pens, ink, parchment, sealing wax and red tape. They also sold books, and

Caxton would take good care that his latest publication was to be seen in the Hall, and in going to and fro from the " Red Pale " we can picture him the centre of an animated group of acquaintances and customers, eager to hear of his work and to offer suggestions.

It may have been in either of these places that the " gentyl and noble esquyer " handed to him the French manuscript of a work on chivalry, with the suggestion that he should print it, which he did under the title of *The Book of the Ordre of Chyvalry*. To this he prefixed his lament that knights did nothing " but go to the bagnios and play dice," and imploring them to spend some of their time in reading about such men as Sir Galahad, Lancelot du Lac, Perse Forest, Gawayne and other famous heroes of chivalry. He accused the knights of his day of " sleeping and taking ease," and pointed out that few of them understood how to manage a horse. The book was in the nature of an elementary treatise, and dealt with such matters as the examination of an esquire who desired to enter the Order, and the significance of the arms belonging to a knight. As it was printed especially for the benefit and instruction of members of the Order, Caxton laid particular stress on the fact that the book was not requisite "to every common man to have," the word "common" in this sense meaning that it was not of general interest. *The Order of Chivalry* is believed to have been printed about the year 1484.

The life of King Arthur, better known as *Le Morte d'Arthur*, was a different book altogether. While dealing with both chivalry and knighthood, it belonged to the class of works called Romances, one of which, *Godfrey of Boloyne*, Caxton had already given to the public. Some of his customers told him that he ought to have printed the life of Arthur first, seeing that he was a man born within this realm, and was the most renowned knight in Christendom. Caxton replied that many persons held the opinion that "ther was no such Arthur," and that all the wonderful feats attributed to him were fables. To this one of his hearers hotly affirmed that such an opinion was folly, and proceeded to give Caxton chapter and verse for the reality of Arthur and his knights of the Round Table. The printer admitted that while he was abroad he had seen and read many books in French dealing with the history of King Arthur, and expressed himself as converted to the belief in his reality. In short, he undertook to print Sir Thomas Malory's work, and prefixed to it a most interesting Prologue, in which he sets out the conversation that led him to print it, and while recommending its perusal to "noble lordes and ladies," he coupled with them "all other estates of the comynaltee of what estate and degree they ben of," clearly indicating that the book was meant for the delight of all and not merely of a class. Caxton divided the text into twenty-one books and one hundred and seven chapters, but this was not done with his usual care, some of the chapters beginning in the middle of a sentence.

The Morte d'Arthur is a splendid folio of 432 leaves, and the printing was finished on July 31st, 1485. The best comment on the popularity of this book is that only two copies are known to exist, and one of these has gone to America, although none of our national libraries possess a copy! Such is our reverence for Caxton.

During the year 1486 Caxton lost his old and valued friend, William Pratt. While it would perhaps be rash to say that they were school-fellows, they had known each other since their prentice days. They were both natives of Kent, they were both mercers, and they were both lovers of books.

Shortly before his death Pratt sent for the printer, and put into his hand a French manuscript, desiring him to translate it into English and print it for the benefit of his countrymen, as it was a work of great merit. Caxton finished the translation a month before his friend died, and called the work *The Book of Good Manners*, which does not convey clearly its nature, as it consisted chiefly of rules and maxims for the good of all classes, and dealt with such topics as chastity, humility, mercy and sobriety. Old age, poverty, marriage and the government of children were also dealt with, and such vices as pride and avarice.

William Pratt died in July, 1486, and his will was proved on the 4th August; but Caxton's name does not occur in it, neither is there any mention of the book, which was finished and printed on the 11th May, 1487. *The Book of Good Manners* was printed with a new fount of type resembling type 3, a Black Letter, believed to have been cut by the same hand as the earlier one, and it has been found bound up with other books printed with the same type. One of these was the *Royal Book* or *Book for a King*, which Caxton had translated three years before from a French work *Le Livre Royal*, at the desire of another (or was it the same?) mercer of London, " a synguler frende of myn." This work was of the same character as *The Book of Good Manners.* The man who lived virtuously is called by the Scriptures a king, and the object of the book was to further virtuous living by the exposure of vice, and amongst its contents were chapters on the ten commandments, the seven deadly sins, the Lord's Prayer, and the cardinal virtues. It was illustrated by a few cuts. There must have been a large demand for works of this kind to have induced Caxton to print these two books, and the *Speculum Vitæ Christi*, all within a few months of one another. Nor was this all. In this same year, 1487, he was evidently commissioned to print a *missal* of the Salisbury use. Either he was too busy, or he felt that it was too large an undertaking for the equipment of the "Red Pale." Accordingly he handed the work over to a printer in Paris called Guillaume Maynyal. Caxton's device appears for the first time in this book. It consisted of his initials divided by an interlaced design, and above and below a border, giving the whole a somewhat Oriental look. All kinds of fanciful suggestions have been made to explain the central design. One was that it represents the figures 74 or 47, and refers to Caxton's age, another that they represented the date of the introduction of printing into England; but Henry Bradshaw of Cambridge was of opinion that the design did not represent Arabic numerals at all, and in the second edition of Blades' *Life*,[1] it is pointed out that it bears a striking resemblance to the merchants' mark of John Felde, mercer, as shown on his brass in Standon Church, Herts, and this seems much more likely, although, until it is found elsewhere than in his books, the question must remain an open one.

[1] *The Biography and Typography of William Caxton*. Second Edition, 1882, p. 139.

CHAPTER VIII

Caxton's last years — Interest of Royal family in his work—The King's librarian—Translated and printed *The Faytte of Armes* for Henry VII—Prints the Statutes—*Blanchardine and Eglantine*—*Eneydos*—Begins translation of the *Vitas Patrum*—His death — Loss of his will — Bequests to St. Margaret's—His influence on his age and on his successors.

IT is sometimes said that Caxton printed more devotional books during the last years of his life than at any other time, and that this was due to a premonition of his approaching end. This is a mistake. Leaving out of account the *Image of Pity* and *The Indulgence* of 1489, both of which were broadsides, some twenty issues came from his press between 1489 and 1491. Of this number nine were second, third and fourth editions of books previously issued, in itself a striking testimony to the printer's judgment of what books were likely to be popular. These reprints were a second edition of the *Speculum Vitæ Christi*, a fourth edition of *The Horæ*, only known to us from a few leaves, a second edition of *Reynard the Fox*, a second edition of *The Directorium Sacerdotum*, a third edition of the *Dictes and Sayings*, and second editions of *The Mirrour of the World*, *The Boke of Courtesy*, *The Festial*, and the *Four Sermons*. Six of the remainder were of a miscellaneous character, including one work on chivalry, three romances, one volume of Statutes, the only thing in the nature of a law-book Caxton ever printed, and one medical work, leaving some seven devotional works, a proportion which is quite in keeping with the output of previous years.

For us the miscellaneous section is the most interesting. The members of the Royal family had at all times proved themselves warm supporters of Caxton and his press. It was under King Edward IV's protection that he set up at Westminster, and King Henry VII was as great a book-collector as his predecessor, and took a pride in adding to the Royal library costly manuscripts and printed books, which he had sumptuously bound in silk and velvet. His librarian was one Quintyn Paulet, who had been keeper of the Royal books since 1464; but of whom, unfortunately, we know nothing beyond what is revealed to us in the Privy Purse Expenses, kept by John Heron, Treasurer of the Chamber, between 1495 and 1505. We should like to think that it was he who summoned Caxton to the King's presence in the early part of the year 1489, and that it was he who brought from the library the French manuscript of Christine de Pisan's *Fait d'Armes et de Chivalry,* which the King handed to Caxton with the request that he would translate it into English and print it without delay. As its title implies, the subject of the book was warlike, and some modern writers have doubted whether a woman could have written such a book; but Christine de Pisan was no ordinary woman, and in the face of her "apology" prefixed to the work, she must be accepted as the writer.

It took Caxton just six months to translate and print *The Faytte of Armes*, which bears the date 14th July, 4th of Hen. VII [i.e., 1489], and he printed it with a new fount of Gothic type, which William Blades erroneously believed to be the last used by him. It very much resembles the type he had used in Bruges and left with Colard Mansion. In the same year he issued the Indulgence above mentioned, issued to help a crusade against the Turks. This was printed in another new fount of type, much smaller than most of Caxton's other types, and with many contractions. Whether or not he was dissatisfied with it, he never used it again, and William Blades stoutly refused to accept it as one of Caxton's founts; but the discovery of its use in side-notes, in a book printed after his death by Wynkyn de Worde, put the matter beyond question.

About this time he also printed with type

No. 6 a small volume of the *Statutes* of the reign of King Henry VII. This was an entirely new departure from the recognized class of books associated with the "Red Pale," and is rather difficult to understand. Perhaps owing to his unfortunate experiences in the law courts of Bruges, Caxton had no high opinion of lawyers, and for that reason perhaps he had left the printing of law-books in the hands of the London printers, Lettou and Machlinia. It is possible that this volume of Statutes was another commission from the King, or it may be that Wynkyn de Worde had persuaded his master to print them. Another point about this book is that these Statutes were printed in English instead of, as was customary, in French.

Another little book which was also very likely printed on the advice of De Worde was *The Governal of Helthe*, the earliest medical book in the English language.

About the same time the King's mother, Margaret, Duchess of Somerset, handed to the printer the French manuscript of a romance called *The History of Blanchardine and Eglantine,* which he had sold her long before, and asked him to translate it into English. This book, which dealt with love and chivalry, was the nearest approach to a modern novel that was known in the fifteen century. When he sold it to her, Caxton knew that it would be likely to please a woman, and she, wishing no doubt to let others share her enjoyment, which those who were unable to read French could not do, she wished it turned into English, and in all probability, at the same time, gave her consent to its being printed. Only one copy of the book is known and that is imperfect.

Equally rare is *The Four Sons of Aymon,* printed about this time. This was another of the popular romances, and like *The History of Blanchardine,* only known from an imperfect copy.

The last work of this character that Caxton undertook was *Eneydos,* a translation from the French of Virgil's *Æneid.* The French work, which was called *Le Livre des Eneydes*, was merely a romance founded upon Virgil's poem.

To this book Caxton prefixed the most delightful and characteristic of all his Prologues, and however feeble his body may have been at this time, it is evident that his mind was as clear and vigorous as ever. He begins by telling us how sitting in his study surrounded by his beloved books, with nothing particular to do, he took down and began to read this French romance. Both the character of the work and the fluency of the language aroused his interest, and in his usual impulsive manner he picked up his pen and fell to translating it into English; but after writing two or three leaves he stopped and became lost in a reverie upon the changes and vicissitudes of the English language. He called to mind that several of his friends had pointed out to him that in some of his translations he had used "over curious terms," and counselled him to use the older and simpler forms of speech that would be more readily understood by the common people. But it appeared to him hard to say which of the many dialects spoken in various parts of England was simple. Not very long before, the Abbot of Westminster had brought him some deeds written in old English and asked him to decipher them; but he found it a task beyond him, the language being more like Dutch than English. From this his memory passed to a humorous incident that had once occurred to a fellow mercer who was on his way to the Continent, but owing to contrary winds was held up in the Downs. Going ashore one day and feeling hungry, he went into a shop or eating-house and called for eggs. The landlady told him that she did not understand French, which made the mercer angry, for he did not understand French either, but wanted her to serve him with eggs. Another of the company thereupon called for "eyren," and was immediately served with eggs. In short, Caxton thought it would be a hard matter to choose between the different dialects, and came to the conclusion that the terms in daily use were the best for his purpose, seeing that the book he was about to translate was likely to be read rather by the intellectual than the "unconnynge" man.

Caxton wound up this Prologue with a graceful tribute to a fellow-worker, the young and rising poet, John Skelton, who had recently been created poet laureate of the University of Oxford. Skelton was a well-known figure at Court, and without doubt the two men were known to each other. It is not unlikely even that Caxton had made overtures to him to be allowed to print some of his work, and had the printer lived a year or two longer no doubt one or other of Skelton's poems would have been printed at the "Red Pale."

The translation of *The Boke of Eneydos* was finished on the 22nd day of June, 1490, and was doubtless printed before the end of the year.

It must have been shortly after finishing *The Eneydos* that Caxton, in this self-same study with the Angel of Death at hand, began the translation of the *Vitas Patrum*.

Meanwhile a succession of small devotional books came from his press. One of these, *The Fifteen Oes*, a quarto volume of prayers, is especially interesting, as being the only one of Caxton's books that were ornamented with wood-cut borders. Each border consisted of four pieces, and eight separate sets of designs were used throughout the book. Spirals of flowers and foliage formed the chief ornament, but in some birds and grotesque animals were introduced, and occasionally a human figure. These blocks have usually been termed wretched specimens of wood-cutting, but this censure is certainly unmerited. They show no little skill on the part both of the artist and the wood-cutter. Some of these cuts show a grotesque human face such as are seen on the misericords of churches and cathedrals. Their clumsy and slovenly appearance was rather the fault of the printer's workman. No attempt was made to space them out in order to make them meet, and not a few were put in upside down.

This little book was made more attractive by the introduction of the full page cut of the Crucifixion, the most artistic block Caxton ever used, which had probably been cut by a French or Italian wood-cutter.

Another little quarto, consisting of only eight leaves, was the *Ars Moriendi that is to saye the craft for to deye for the helthe of mannes soule,* perhaps translated from the Latin by Caxton.

What is believed to have been the last book that came from his press was *The Book of Divers Ghostly Matters*, a quarto of 148 leaves, consisting of three separate tracts, *The Orologium Sapientiæ, The Twelve Profits of Tribulation* and *The Rule of St. Benet,* printed at the desire of certain worshipful persons.

The end came suddenly. Caxton had reached the last page of his translation of the *Vitas Patrum.* The author had been showing that the house of God was a just and rightful heart. The foundations were faith, the height hope, the breadth and size charity, the sides perseverance and concord, and so on, and concludes: "God thenne give us his grace to find in us such an house that it may please him to lodge therein to the end that in this world he keep us from adversity spiritual. And in the end of our days he bring us with him in to his Royame [i.e., realme] of heaven for to be partyners of the glorye eternal, the which grant to us the holy trynyte. Amen."

These were the last words Caxton wrote. Whether he died immediately after writing them, or was then seized with sudden illness and died shortly afterwards, is unknown; he was dead before the day was out. Wynkyn de Worde bore testimony that the translation of the *Vitas Patrum* was finished by William Caxton "at the last daye of his lyff." Could any end have been more fitting?

If he was born about the year 1424 he would have been sixty-seven at the time of his death, not by any means a great age. But he may not have been a robust man, and he had used both mind and body vigorously. For thirty years he had followed his trade of a mercer on the Continent, and had weighty matters to deal with, which necessitated much travelling; while for the last fifteen years he had spent his energies in the management of his printing office and the translating and editing of books. Exactly one hundred have been traced as having been printed either by him or for him during that time, and from the fact that many of these are only known by a few leaves recovered from old bindings, it seems certain that we do not know the full extent of the output of the "Red Pale."

Judged from the technical side, Caxton's work as a printer bears no comparison with the finished work of his continental brethren, such as Erhard Ratdolt of Venice or Verard of Paris. He did not try to emulate them. His object in bringing a printing-press to this country was the increasing of knowledge amongst his countrymen by multiplying copies of the best literature by means of the new art. To get it printed was the great thing, it did not matter in the least whether the books had title pages or illustrations. From the number which he translated and edited during this time it seems impossible that he could have given much time to the mechanical part of the work. Nor was there much necessity for him to do so after his foreman, Wynkyn de Worde, became more experienced as a printer and more used to the ideas and wishes of his master. Master and workman understood one another, this is evident from the fact that, so far as we know, neither wished to make any change. There is little doubt that within a few years of the establishment of the printing house Caxton left the management of the purely mechanical work, all that related to the actual printing of the books and the management of the workmen, to De Worde. No doubt when Caxton passed a manuscript to him he signified his wishes as to the format, whether folio, quarto or octavo, and they talked over together the type to be used, whether the work was to be illustrated, and if so, how, and also the number of copies that were to form an edition. Caxton again probably corrected his own proofs and pointed out any other errors in the press-work that happened to catch his eye, but all such details as pagination, signatures, head-lines, or the correct placing of illustrations, he concerned himself little about, so long as the text was correctly printed. Now Wynkyn de Worde was never at any time what would be called a good printer. He was careless and slovenly, and where such faults show themselves in Caxton's books, we may feel sure that they were due to Wynkyn de Worde rather than his employer.

Caxton was much more interested in the literary side of his work, in choosing the books that were to be printed. In this, as we have seen, he was greatly helped by his friends who were book lovers. Professor Lathrop would have us believe that he did nothing without first calculating the cost, and only venturing to print a book of a certain class, when some previous book of the same kind had proved a success. Anything more utterly at variance with Caxton's character and aims it is difficult to conceive. Was he thinking of his own profit when he translated the *Recueil,* or when at his "grete charge and dispense" he went to Cologne to learn the art of printing? Had he no higher aim than his own self-interest when he printed Gower's *Confessio Amantis* and Chaucer's *Canterbury Tales?* Was it merely for the money that they brought him that he translated *The Mirrour of the World* and *The Book of Good Manners* for his two friends, Hugh Brice and William Pratt? I hope and believe that not many Englishmen will be found to endorse Professor Lathrop's estimate of Caxton and his work.

If William Caxton had done no more than introduce the printing-press into England and had printed nothing more than bill-heads and ballads he would deserve all the honour Englishmen can pay him, and they would still be in his debt.

Of Caxton's private life we know very little. We know that he left a daughter, Elizabeth, who was married to a tailor named Gerard Croppe. The marriage was a failure, and she obtained a separation from him, and it was agreed that Croppe was to have twenty printed legends at 13s. 4d. apiece as part of Caxton's bequest.

It is also known that Caxton made a will; but in spite of strenuous search at Somerset House and amongst the records at Westminster it has never been found. It could not fail to be of the highest interest, because what we do know of its contents entitles us to believe that what we do not know would be equally valuable.

Somewhere about 1493, Gerard Croppe, Caxton's son-in-law, brought an action against Sir Richard Warde, priest, who is named as one of Caxton's executors, in respect of a legacy of £80, which Croppe declared had been left to him by the printer, but which his executors refused to pay. Again in Michaelmas Term, 12 Hen. VII, at the suit of Robert Redknapp, mercer, perhaps another of Caxton's executors, an inquiry was ordered by the Court of King's Bench into Croppe's means, evidently with a view to distraint, he having infringed the Statute "de Conspiratoribus." Altogether Gerard Croppe seems to have made things as unpleasant as he well could for the executors, and as the above arbitration award was not delivered until 1495-96, and the law court proceedings are of about the same date, we may infer that there was considerable delay, something like four or five years, before probate of Caxton's will was granted.

Having no heir, Caxton is believed to have left his business to his late foreman, Wynkyn de Worde, and this belief receives some support from the small output of books that came from the "Red Pale" during the years that immediately succeeded Caxton's death. If the business was mentioned in the will, De Worde could do very little until it was legally proved.

Amongst his other bequests, Caxton left a considerable number of *Legenda* to the churchwardens of St. Margaret's, Westminster. It used to be thought that these were copies of the *Golden Legend* printed in 1484; but it seems much more likely that they were copies of the *Legenda* which Caxton commissioned William Maynyal to print for him in Paris about 1487. This which was more in the nature of a service-book for the Church, would have sold for about the price 6s. 8d., which was the sum received by the churchwardens for some of the copies in their possession; but it is difficult to understand why Gerard Croppe had to pay 13s. 4d. each for his copies, unless they were copies of the *Golden Legend,* the wholesale price of which was 24s. each.

That Caxton had made his printing office pay, and that he was in comfortable circumstances when he died, there is no reason to doubt. The fees paid at his burial were more than those usually paid, which may or may not have been evidence of his being in a good financial position. In considering this point we must not forget that he took his share of parish duties, and there is no doubt that he was held in great esteem and respect, not only by the parishioners of St. Margaret's, but also by the Abbot and clergy of Westminster, and they may have desired to mark this by giving him something in the nature of a public funeral. So that it does not do to jump hastily to the conclusion that he was a rich man.

There were two strongly marked traits in Caxton's character, his piety and his love of his country. His respect for Earl Rivers was due to the Earl's pious and charitable acts. In his choice of books he was guided largely by their moral tone, and he invariably wound up his introductory matter with a prayer for the blessing of God on his work, and his last great undertaking dealt with the lives of holy men and women.

Caxton's love for England was a feature of his life. There were no men to his thinking who were the equals of Englishmen; no citizens in the world like the citizens of London. He never picked up a book in a foreign language but he wanted to translate it into English for the benefit of his countrymen. Chaucer he considered the greatest of all poets. He crowned his lifework by introducing the printing-press into England in order that Englishmen, through the medium of good literature, might rise to higher things.

CHAPTER IX

Caxton as translator, editor and author—His Prologues and Epilogues—Value of his work as a roadmaker.

THE introduction of the printing-press into England was, after all, but a small part of the boon that Caxton conferred upon his countrymen.

The work required much material, and it was by finding the right kind of material that he has earned his position as a roadmaker. As we have already said, if he had done no more than print bill-heads he would deserve all the honour we could pay him; but our debt to him is infinitely greater, for by his choice of the highest class of literature he laid the road to greater knowledge, and awakened a taste for reading that has grown with the centuries. It is maintained by some, that he merely gratified the tastes of a small circle of aristocratic readers by printing what they wanted; but it has already been shown that such was not the case, but that he catered for all who could read. Take a few of his own statements on this subject. In his very first book, *The Recuyell of the Histories of Troy,* he appeals to "all them that shall read this said work." In *The Chess Book* he says: "But to the intent that others of what estate or degree he or they stand in may see in this little book," etc.

Earl Rivers wished *The Cordial* "to be printed and so multiplied to go abroad among the people." *The Knight of the Tower* was necessary to every gentleman or gentlewoman "of whatever estate." To say that he did not guide the world to the best literature because it was already known to the few is a poor argument, which overlooks the fact that, like a stone thrown in a pond, the benefits of his work as printer and translator spread in ever-widening circles that reached shores that he never dreamed of.

Caxton's work as a translator was of even

greater value than his work as a printer. Much of the best literature was only to be had in French, and long before he ever thought of learning to print he had been moved to translate books into the English tongue. Translating was more or less a hobby with him, and he seems to have begun at a fairly early age. He probably translated many things that never appeared in print.

The earliest of his translations that we know of was the Flemish and French phrase-book, which we may assume him to have bought soon after his arrival in Flanders in 1441, and the translation of which from French into English furnished him with some amusement at odd moments. It was probably finished some time before he met with the copy of *The Recuyell* that so aroused his interest and was destined to have such far-reaching results.

Caxton was well equipped for his self-imposed task of translating and editing books. He has put it on record that his parents gave him a good education. Now a "good" education in the fifteenth century was only open to the wealthier classes, and it implied something more than was obtainable by the horn-book. In spite of his self-depreciation—of his oft repeated lament of his want of "connyng" and of his "rude and simple" English—he had no cause to be ashamed of his knowledge of his native tongue. His English was terse and vigorous in spite of a somewhat involved style, and what one of his editors calls his "tiresome tautology," faults that were common to other writers of that age.

He was thoroughly conversant with the French language. The ground-work of this he may have got at school. Although he tells us that he was never in France, the French language was spoken freely on the Continent, and French literature was more common than that of almost any other country, while during his thirty years residence abroad he must have learnt to converse freely in that language. For the same reason he must have been equally well acquainted with both Flemish and Dutch. Latin he would certainly have acquired at school, as it was part of the curriculum of the medieval schools. Moreover, as Governor of the English Nation in Bruges, a knowledge of that language was essential, as most treaties and all correspondence were carried on in Latin. Besides, he could not have printed service books and indulgences, missals and books of hours, all of which were in Latin, without being able to correct the copy and detect misprints. It is true that he may have employed a "reader" to see Latin books through the press; but in *The Life of Saynt Rockes*, which is part of the *Golden Legend*, he distinctly states that it "is translated oute of latyn into English by me William Caxton," and he was not the man to lay claim to a work done by someone else. Moreover, he is believed to have translated from the Latin *The Declamation of Noblesse*, which forms the third section of the *Tully on Old Age,* which drew words of praise from Leland.

Caxton must have translated quickly. In the seventeen years during which he was at work as a printer he translated between twenty and thirty books, the majority of them from the French, and some of them, like the *Golden Legend*, contained seven or eight hundred folio pages. As he was probably subject to all kinds of interruption, and at times was held up by the difficulties of the text, not much is gained by knowing that *The Mirrour of the World* took him ten weeks to translate, and *Godefroy of Boloyne* twelve weeks.

To convey the meaning of the original was his great aim. He tells us over and over again that he had followed his author as nearly as he could, not changing the sentence nor adding nor taking away anything; but his translations were always free, and he even transferred French words bodily when he did not readily find an English word to suit him.

Coming now to his work as editor, we find him equally busy. He edited every book that passed through his press, that is to say he not only "oversaw" the text, but he added to most of them a Prologue or introduction and an Epilogue or final statement. His chief difficulty lay with his own language. In the *Polychronicon* he turned the old English of Trevisa's day into the speech of his own day, and in the *Eneydos* he tells us that in his judgment the common terms that were in daily use were easier to understand than the old English. Whether he was right is a matter of opinion. The editors of the *Cambridge History of English Literature* do not think he was. They say that very often his rendering spoilt more vigorous narrative. In the Prologue to *Charles the Great,* Caxton excuses himself for not using "gay termes" nor subtle eloquence on the ground that his aim was to give a translation that would be understood by all his readers. He admitted that he had not the knowledge or skill in words of Chaucer, Lydgate or Skelton; but how anxious he was at all times to put the best text into print is shown by his annoyance when he found out that his first edition of *The Canterbury Tales* had been printed from an imperfect and corrupt copy.

Caxton's Prologues and Epilogues add very much to the value of his work. In a few instances, as in *The Life of Charles the Great* and *The Chess Book,* he was content to translate the Prologues of his authors; but even in these we get many personal details. In the remainder his wide reading, his insight into character, his humour, his scorn of idleness and effeminacy, his piety, and lastly his loyalty, are mirrored faithfully. No better example can be found than those that accompany his first book, *The Recuyell of the History of Troy,* in which he sets out at length how he was moved to begin it, of the difficulties he met with, his meeting with Margaret, Duchess of Burgundy, and her enthusiasm and help. How the work was continued at Ghent and

Cologne, how he learnt the art of printing because his pen was worn, his hand weary and his eye dim with looking on the white paper.

Equally interesting are those which precede and follow his edition of the *De Senectute*, in which he tells of the difficulty and expense of procuring a copy, how he came to add to it the translation of the *De Amicia* by the Earl of Worcester, and his lament for that nobleman's death.

How his humour crops out in the *Dictes and Sayings* and in *Eneydos* has already been noticed, while the story of the honest priest who rebuked his bishop, which he appended to his translation of *Æsop*, is only one of a hundred instances of his piety.

That he was a staunch adherent to the House of York is evident from his Epilogue to *The Mirrour of the World*, and his frequent reference in other books to the King's "protection." At the same time he was equally loyal to Henry VII when circumstances placed that monarch on the throne.

Two things alone mar these Prologues, and one is what I have already termed Caxton's exaggerated lip-service to Royality and the nobility. It was a survival of the old feudalism, and was the fashion of the time. It is not to be taken seriously. His other fault is undue repetition. He constantly repeats in the Epilogue what he has already said in the Prologue. In *The Mirrour of the World* he tells us twice over that it was undertaken at the wish of Hugh Brice, alderman and citizen of London, who wished to present it to Lord Hastings, and many passages are not free from that "tiresome tautology" already referred to.

Nevertheless, they give us many biographical details, and show us the working of his mind, for which we may be grateful.

The value of Caxton's work as a roadmaker cannot be summed up better than in the words of a writer of the last century :

"It is to the easy and cheap methods of

communicating thought from man to man, which enable a country to sift, as it were, its whole people, and to produce in its science, its literature and its arts, not the brightest efforts of a limited class, but the highest exertions of the most powerful minds among a whole community—it is this that has given birth to the wide-spreading civilization of the present day, and which promises a futurity yet more prolific. Whoever is acquainted with the present state of science and the mechanical arts, and looks back over the inventions and civilization which the fourteen centuries subsequent to the introduction of Christianity have produced, and compares them with the advance made during the succeeding four centuries following the invention of printing, will have no doubt as to the effective cause."

That the printing-press would sooner or later have been established in England is certain; but it is well for the country that it was brought over by such a man as William

Caxton, who put the fear of God and the good of his country before all other considerations, and who laid on a solid foundation the road which has led us to such high and noble results.

PRINCIPAL DATES

1424 (?) Approximate date of birth.

1438 Apprentice to Robert Large.

1439 Peace signed between England and Flanders.

1441 Death of Robert Large.
Caxton goes abroad.

1453 Brief visit to England. Admitted to Livery of Mercers' Company.

1462-3 Elected Governor of English merchants at Bruges.

1464 Caxton appointed by Royal Commission to confer with Duke of Burgundy.

1467 Death of Philip the Good and succession of Charles the Bold as Duke of Burgundy.

1468 Marriage of Charles the Bold and Princess Margaret, sister of King Edward IV. Caxton appointed one of the ambassadors to treat with Charles for commercial treaty.

1468 Caxton began to translate Raoul le Fevre's *Le Recueil des Histoires de Troye.*

1470 Caxton enters the service of Margaret, Duchess of Burgundy. Tells her of his attempt to translate *The Recueil.*

1471 Caxton in Cologne.

1473 Caxton returned to Bruges and set up as a printer with Colard Mansion.

1474 (?) Approximate date of printing of *The Recuyell of the Historyes of Troye,* the first book printed in the English language.

1476 Caxton returned to England and set up a printing-press within the precincts of the Abbey of Westminster.

1477 First book with a date printed in England by Caxton.

1481 Illustrations first used by Caxton in *The Mirrour of the World.*

1484 (?) Approximate date of the printing of the *Golden Legend,* the largest book that came from Caxton's press.

1487 Caxton's device first found in the *Sarum Missal* issued in that year.

1491 (?) Approximate date of Caxton's death.

24
67

BOOKS RECOMMENDED

ÆSOP, THE FABLES OF, as first printed by William Caxton in 1484, with those of Avian, Alfonso and Poggio. Edited by J. Jacobs. 2 parts. 1889.

AMES, JOSEPH. Typographical Antiquities. Edited by W. Herbert. 3 vols. 1785. Edited by T. F. Dibdin. 3 vols. 1810.

APOLLYN OF THYRE. The Romance of Kynge. Reproduced in facsimile by E. W. Ashbee. 1870.

ARBER, EDWARD. An English Garner. 1903.

ARNOLD, RICHARD. Customs of London, otherwise called Arnold's Chronicle. Edited by F. Douce. 1811.

AYMON. The right plesaunt and goodly historie of the foure sonnes of Aymon. Englisht from the French by W. Caxton. Early English Text Society. Extra Series. Vol. XLIV. 1884.

BLADES, WM. Biography and Typography of Caxton. 2 vols. 1877. How to Tell a Caxton. 1870.

BLANCHARDYN AND EGLANTINE. E.E.T.S. Extra Series. LVIII. Edited by L. Kellner.

BRADSHAW, HENRY. Notice of a fragment of the Fifteen Oes. 1877.

BRITISH MUSEUM. Catalogue of English Books to 1640 3 vols.

CAXTON CELEBRATION. Catalogue of Exhibits. 1877.

CHARLES THE GREAT. English Charlemagne Romances, parts 3 and 4. 1880-81. Edited by S. J. Herrtage.

CHESSE, GAME AND PLAYE OF THE. 1474. Verbatim reprint of first edition. Edited by W. E. A. Axon. 1883.

CHIVALRY, ORDER OF. Translated from the French by W. Caxton. Edited by F. S. Ellis. Kelmscott Press, Hammersmith. 1892.

CHRISTINE DE PISAN. Morale Proverbes. Edited by William Blades. 1859.

CUNNINGHAM, S. Story of William Caxton.

CURIAL MADE BY MAYSTER ALAIN CHARRETIER. Translated by William Caxton. Collated with the French original by Paul Meyer, and edited by F. J. Furnivall. E.E.T.S. Extra Series. LIV. 1888.

CURTESYE, BOOK OF. Edited by F. J. Furnivall. E.E.T.S. Extra Series. III. 1868.

DIALOGUES IN FRENCH AND ENGLISH. Edited by H. Bradley. E.E.T.S. Extra Series. LXXIX. 1900.

DICTES AND SAYINGS OF THE PHILOSOPHERS. A facsimile reproduction. Edited by William Blades. 1877.

DUFF, E. GORDON. Century of the English Book Trade. 1905. Commemoracio Lamentacionis sive compassionis Beate Marie. Reproduced in facsimile from the unique copy printed at Westminster by William Caxton. 1901.

Early English Printing, Facsimiles of Types. 1896.

Fifteenth Century English Books. 1917.

Horæ B.V.M. secundum usuon Sarum. 1908.

Printers of Westminster and London. 1906.

William Caxton. Chicago.

ENEYDOS. Edited by M. T. Culley and F. J. Furnivall. E.E.T.S. Extra Series. LVII. 1890.

GODEFFROY OF BOLOYNE. Translated from the French by W. Caxton. Edited by M. N. Colvin, Ph.D. E.E.T.S. Extra Series. LXIV. 1893.

GOLDEN LEGEND. Edited by F. S. Ellis. 3 vols. Kelmscott Press. 1892.
—— Edited by F. S. Ellis. 7 vols. 1900.
—— By P. Butler, Baltimore. 1899.

GOWER, JOHN. English Works. 2 vols. E.E.T.S. Extra Series. LXXXI–LXXXII.

HELYAS. Knight of the Swan. Thom's Collection of Early Prose Romances. Vol. III. 1828.

KNIGHT, CHARLES. William Caxton. 1877.

LEWIS, J. Life of Caxton. 1737.

OVID. Six bookes of Metamorphoses. Trans. out of Frensshe by William Caxton. Edited by G. Hibbert. Roxburghe Club. XXVI. 1819.

PARIS AND VIENNE. Edited by W. C. Hazlitt. 1868.

PLOMER, HENRY R. Short History of English Printing. 2nd edition. 1915.

POLLARD, A. W. Fifteenth Century Prose and Verse. 1883.

RECUYELL OF THE HISTORYES OF TROYES. Edited by H. Sommer. 2 vols. 1894.

REYNARD THE FOX. Translated and printed by Caxton. Edited by E. Arber. English Scholars' Library. I. 1880.

RICCI, S. DE. Census of Caxtons.

UPDIKE, D. B. Printing Types. 2 vols. Camb., Mass. 1922.

WARD, A. W., AND WALLER, A. R. Cambridge History of English Literature. Vol. II, pp. 332 *et seq.* 1907.

INDEX